STYLE

The Basics of Clarity and Grace

Second Edition

Joseph M. Williams
The University of Chicago

PEARSON
Longman

New York Boston San Francisco
London Toronto Sydney Tokyo Singapore Madrid
Mexico City Munich Paris Cape Town Hong Kong Montreal

Senior Sponsoring Editor: Virginia L. Blanford
Senior Supplements Editor: Donna Campion
Senior Marketing Manager: Alexandra Rivas-Smith
Managing Editor: Bob Ginsberg
Production Manager: Joseph Vella
Project Coordination, Text Design, and Electronic Page Makeup:
    Thompson Steele, Inc.
Senior Cover Design Manager: Nancy Danahy
Cover Design Manager/Designer: John Callahan
Manufacturing Manager/Buyer: Mary Fischer
Printer and Binder: Courier Corp.—Westford
Cover Printer: Phoenix Color Corp.

Text credit: From "The Aims of Education" in *The Aims of Education and Other Essays* by Alfred North Whitehead. Copyright © 1929 by Macmillan Publishing Co., Inc., renewed 1957 by Evelyn Whitehead. Reprinted by permission.

Library of Congress Cataloging-in-Publication Data
    Williams, Joseph M.
      Style : the basics of clarity and grace / Joseph M. Williams.—2nd ed.
        p. cm.
      Includes index.
      ISBN 0-321-33085-4
      1. English language—Rhetoric. 2. English language—Technical
    English. 3. English language—Business English. 4. English language—
    Style. 5. Technical writing. 6. Business writing. I. Title.
    PE1421.W5455 2005
    808'.042—dc22
                                                                    2005000458

Copyright © 2006 by Pearson Education, Inc.

All rights reserved. No part of this publication may be reproduced, stored in a retrieval system, or transmitted, in any form or by any means, electronic, mechanical, photocopying, recording, or otherwise, without the prior written permission of the publisher. Printed in the United States.

Please visit our website at http://www.ablongman.com

ISBN 0-321-33085-4

    3 4 5 6 7 8 9 10—CRW—08 07 06

To my mother and father

*. . . English style, familiar but not coarse,
elegant, but not ostentatious . . .*
—SAMUEL JOHNSON

Contents

Preface

Most people won't realize that writing is a craft.
You have to take your apprenticeship in it like anything else.
—KATHERINE ANNE PORTER

THE SECOND EDITION

What's New

In this second edition of *Style the Basics,* I've reorganized parts of some lessons to make them flow more logically and imposed on most of the lessons a three-part structure of *Understanding, Diagnosis and Revision,* and *Summing Up*. Both changes should help readers move through those lessons more easily. I replaced examples in Lessons Five and Six and, as always, did a good deal of line editing throughout.

What's the Same

This second edition aims at answering the same questions I asked in the first one:

- What is it in a sentence that makes readers judge it as they do?
- How can we diagnose our own prose to anticipate their judgments?
- How can we revise a sentence so that readers will think better of it?

The standard advice about writing ignores those questions. It is mostly truisms like "Make a plan" and "Think of your audience"—advice that most of us ignore as we wrestle ideas out onto the page. When I first drafted this paragraph, I wasn't thinking about you; I was struggling to get my own ideas straight. What I did know was that I would come back to this paragraph again and again, and that it was likely to be only then—as I revised—that I could think about you and discover the plan that fit my draft. I also knew that as I did so, there were some principles I could rely on. This book explains them.

PRINCIPLES, NOT PRESCRIPTIONS

Those principles may seem prescriptive, but that's not how I intend them. I offer them as ways to help you predict how readers will judge your prose and then help you decide whether and how to revise it. As you learn all those principles, you may find that you write more slowly. That's inevitable. Whenever we reflect on what we do as we do it, we become self-conscious, sometimes to the point of paralysis. It passes. You can avoid some of that paralysis if you remember that these principles have little to do with how you draft, much to do with how you revise. If there is a first principle of drafting, it's to forget advice about how to do it.

Some Prerequisites

To learn how to revise efficiently, though, you have to know a few things:

- You should know a few grammatical terms: subject, verb, noun, active, passive, clause, preposition, and coordination.
- You will have to learn new meanings for two familiar words: topic and stress.
- You will need five terms that you probably don't know. Two are important: nominalization and metadiscourse; three are useful: resumptive modifier, summative modifier, and free modifier.

Finally, if you are reading this book on your own, go slowly. It is not an amiable essay to read in a sitting or two. Take the lessons a few pages at a time, edit someone else's writing, then some of your own written a few weeks ago, then something you've written that day.

If you find these principles useful, and would like a text that offers a fuller discussion of style as well as revision exercises, a longer version of *Style* is available. *Style: Ten Lessons in Clarity and Grace,* Eighth Edition, can be ordered using ISBN 0-321-28831-9.

SUPPLEMENTS

To see a complete list of supplements available upon adoption of this text, please visit this book's online catalog page, which is accessible from www.ablongman.com.

ACKNOWLEDGMENTS

So many have offered support, suggestions, and criticisms over the last twenty-five years, that I cannot thank you all. I have learned from undergraduate, graduate and professional students, and post-docs who have gone through the Little Red Schoolhouse writing program at the University of Chicago (a.k.a. Advanced Academic and Professional Writing). I am equally grateful to the graduate students who taught these principles and offered important feedback.

For several years, I have had the good fortune to work with two people who have been both good colleagues and good friends and whose careful thinking has helped me think better about many matters, both professional and personal: Don Freeman and Greg Colomb. Don's careful readings have saved me from more than a few howlers. For more than twenty-five years now, Greg has put up with more than most friends would, and I have benefited from both his scrupulous critical thinking and our intemperate shouting matches. It has been a pleasure and a privilege to work with him and to travel and hang out with him and Sandra.

And again, those who contribute more to my life than I let them know: Oliver, Chris, and Ingrid; Dave, Patty, Owen, and Matilde; Megan, Phil, and Lily; Joe, Christine, Nicholas, and Katherine. And at beginning and end still, Joan, whose patience and love still flow more generously than I deserve.

JOSEPH M. WILLIAMS

Understanding Style

Have something to say,
and say it as clearly as you can.
That is the only secret of style.
—MATTHEW ARNOLD

CLARITY AND UNDERSTANDING

This book rests on two principles: it is good to write clearly, and anyone can. The first is self-evident, especially to those who have to read a lot of writing like this:

> An understanding of the causal factors involved in excessive drinking by students could lead to their more effective treatment.

But that second principle may seem optimistic to those who try to write more clearly, but can't get close to this:

> We could more effectively treat students who drink excessively if we understood why they do.

Of course, writing fails for reasons more serious than unclear sentences. We bewilder readers when we can't organize complex ideas coherently, and we can't expect their assent when we ignore their reasonable questions and objections. But once we've formulated our claims, organized supporting reasons, and grounded them on sound evidence, we must still express it all in clear, direct sentences, a difficult task for most writers and a daunting one for many.

It is a problem that has afflicted generations of writers who have hidden their ideas not only from their readers, but sometimes even from themselves. When we read that kind of writing in government regulations, we call it *bureaucratese;* when we read it in legal documents, *legalese;* in academic writing that inflates small ideas into gassy abstractions, *academese.* Written deliberately or carelessly, it's a language of exclusion that a democracy can't tolerate. It is a problem with a long history. Unfortunately, it is a style so common that it has become an institutional standard.

The Irresistible Lure of Obscurity

In the best-known essay on modern English style, "Politics and the English Language," George Orwell anatomized the pretentious language of politicians and academics:

> The keynote [of a pretentious style] is the elimination of simple verbs. Instead of being a single word, such as *break, stop, spoil, mend, kill,* a verb becomes a phrase, made up of a noun or adjective tacked on to some general-purposes verb such as *prove, serve, form, play, render.* In addition, the passive voice is wherever possible used in preference to the active, and noun constructions are used instead of gerunds (*by examination* of instead of *by examining*).

But in abusing that style Orwell adopted it. He could have written more concisely:

> Pretentious writers eliminate simple verbs. Instead of using one word, such as *break, stop, kill,* they turn a verb into a noun or adjective, then tack it on to a general-purpose verb such as *prove, serve, form, play, render.* Wherever they can, they use the passive voice instead of the active and noun constructions instead of gerunds (*by examination* instead of *by examining*).

If the best-known critic of a turgid style could not resist it, we shouldn't be surprised that politicians and academics embrace it. On the language of the social sciences:

> A turgid and polysyllabic prose does seem to prevail in the social sciences. . . . Such a lack of ready intelligibility, I believe, usually has little or nothing to do with the complexity of thought. It has to

do almost entirely with certain confusions of the academic writer about his own status.

—C. Wright Mills, *The Sociological Imagination*

On the language of medicine:

It now appears that obligatory obfuscation is a firm tradition within the medical profession. . . . [Medical writing] is a highly skilled, calculated attempt to confuse the reader. . . . A doctor feels he might get passed over for an assistant professorship because he wrote his papers too clearly—because he made his ideas seem too simple.

—Michael Crichton, *New England Journal of Medicine*

On the language of law:

In law journals, in speeches, in classrooms and in courtrooms, lawyers and judges are beginning to worry about how often they have been misunderstood, and they are discovering that sometimes they can't even understand each other.

—Tom Goldstein, *New York Times*

On the language of science:

There are times when the more the authors explain [about ape communication], the less we understand. Apes certainly seem capable of using language to communicate. Whether scientists are remains doubtful.

—Douglas Chadwick, *New York Times*

Most of us first confront that kind of unclear writing in textbook sentences like this one:

Recognition of the fact that systems [of grammar] differ from one language to another can serve as the basis for serious consideration of the problems confronting translators of the great works of world literature originally written in a language other than English.

In about half as many words, that means,

When we recognize that languages have different grammars, we can consider the problems of those who translate great works of literature into English.

Generations of students have struggled with dense writing, many thinking they were not smart enough to grasp a writer's deep ideas. Some have been right about that, but more could have blamed the writer's inability (or refusal) to write clearly. Many students, sad to say, give up; sadder still, others learn not only to read that style but to write it, inflicting it on the next generation of readers, thereby sustaining a 400-year-old tradition of opaque prose.

SOME PRIVATE CAUSES OF UNCLEAR WRITING

But if unclear writing has a long social history, it also has private causes. Michael Crichton mentioned one: some writers plump up their prose to impress those who confuse a difficult style with deep thinking. And when we don't know what we're talking about (or have no confidence in what we do know) we typically throw up a tangle of abstract words in long, complex sentences.

Others write graceless prose not deliberately but because they are seized by the idea that writing is good only when it's free of errors only a grammarian can explain. They approach a blank page not as a place to explore new ideas, but as a minefield to cross gingerly. They creep from word to word, concerned less with their readers' understanding than with their own survival.

Others write unclearly because they just freeze up, especially when they are learning to think and write in a new academic or professional setting. Those afflicted include not just undergraduates taking their first course in economics or psychology, but graduate students, businesspeople, doctors, lawyers—anyone writing on a new topic for unfamiliar and therefore intimidating readers. As we struggle to master new and complex ideas, most of us write worse than we do when we write about things we understand better. If that sounds like you, take heart. You will write more clearly once you more clearly understand your subject and readers.

But the biggest reason we write unclearly is our ignorance of how others read our writing. What we write always seems clearer to us than it does to our readers, because we can read into it what we want readers to get out of it. And so instead of revising our writing to meet their needs, we send it off as soon as it meets ours.

In all of this, of course, there is a great irony: we are likely to confuse others when we write about a subject that confuses us. But when we also read about a complex subject written in a complex style, we too easily assume that such complexity signals deep thought, and so we try to imitate it, compounding our already confused writing.

This book shows you how to avoid that, how to read your own writing as others will, and, when you should, how to make it better.

ON WRITING AND REWRITING

A warning: if you think about these principles *as you draft,* you may never draft anything. Most experienced writers get something down on paper or up on the screen as fast as they can, just to have something to revise. Then as they rewrite an early draft into something clearer, they more clearly understand their ideas. And when they understand their ideas better, they express them more clearly, and when they express them more clearly, they understand them even better . . . and so it goes, until they run out of energy, interest, or time.

For a fortunate few, that moment comes weeks, months, even years after they begin. (Over the last twenty-five years, I've wrestled this book through dozens of drafts, and there are still parts I can't get right.) For most of us, though, the deadline is closer to tomorrow morning. And so we have to settle for prose that is less than perfect, but as good as we can make it. (Perfection is the ideal, but the enemy of done.) So use what you find here not as rules to impose on every sentence *as* you draft it, but as principles to help you identify sentences likely to give your readers a problem, and then to revise those sentences quickly.

As important as clarity is, though, some occasions call for more:

> Now the trumpet summons us again—not as a call to bear arms, though arms we need; not as a call to battle, though embattled we are; but a call to bear the burden of a long twilight struggle, year in and year out, "rejoicing in hope, patient in tribulation," a struggle against the common enemies of man: tyranny, poverty, disease and war itself.

> —John F. Kennedy, Inaugural Address, January 20, 1961

Few of us are called upon to write a presidential address, but in even our modest prose, some of us take a private pleasure in writing a shapely sentence, regardless of whether anyone will notice, like the cabinetmaker who sands the back of a drawer. Those who enjoy not just writing a sentence but crafting it will find suggestions in Lesson Nine. Writing is also a social act that might or might not serve the best interests of readers, so in Lesson Ten, I address some ethical issues of style.

Many years ago, H. L. Mencken wrote this:

> With precious few exceptions, all the books on style in English are by writers quite unable to write. The subject, indeed, seems to exercise a special and dreadful fascination over school ma'ams, bucolic college professors, and other such pseudoliterates. . . . Their central aim, of course, is to reduce the whole thing to a series of simple rules—the overmastering passion of their melancholy order, at all times and everywhere.

Mencken was right: no one learns to write well by rule, especially those who can't feel or think or see. But I know that many who do see clearly, feel deeply, and think carefully can't write sentences that make their thoughts, feelings, and visions clear to others. I also know that the more clearly we write, the more clearly we see and feel and think. Rules help no one do that, but some principles can.

Here they are.

Lesson

2

Correctness

*No grammatical rules have sufficient authority
to control the firm and established usage of language.
Established custom, in speaking and writing,
is the standard to which we must at last resort
for determining every controverted point
in language and style.*
—HUGH BLAIR

CORRECTNESS, CHOICE, AND OBEDIENCE

To a careful writer, nothing is more important than choice, but in some matters, we have none—we can't put *the* after a noun, as in *street the*. But we choose when we can. For example, which of these sentences would you choose to write if you wanted readers to think you wrote clearly?

1. Lack of newspaper support caused our loss of the election.
2. We lost the election because newspapers didn't support us.

Both are grammatically "correct," but most of us choose (2).

Unlike clarity, though, correctness seems a matter not of choice, but of obedience. When the *American Heritage Dictionary* says that *irregardless* is "never acceptable" (except, they say, for humor), our freedom to choose it seems at best academic. In matters of this kind, we choose not between better

and worse, but between right and utterly, irredeemably, un-
equivocally Wrong, which is, of course, no choice at all.

But that lack of choice does seem to simplify things: "Correctness" requires not good judgment but only a good memory.
If we remember that *irregardless* is always Wrong, it ought not
rise to even a subconscious level of choice. Some teachers and
editors think we should memorize dozens of other such "rules":

- Don't begin a sentence with *and* or *but*.

- Don't use double negatives.

- Don't split infinitives.

Unfortunately, it's more complicated than that. Some rules
are real rules: we must obey them or be labeled at least un-
schooled. But a handful of other often repeated rules are less
important than many think (some are based on a grammarian's
whim). If you obsess over them, you will keep yourself from
writing quickly and clearly. In fact, that's why I address "correctness" now, before clarity, because I want to put it where it
belongs—behind us.

THREE KINDS OF RULES

Corrosive social attitudes about correctness have been encouraged by generations of grammarians who, in their zeal to codify
"good" English, have confused three kinds of "rules":

1. Some rules—call them the "Real Rules"—define what makes
   English—articles precede nouns: *the book*, not *book the*.
   Speakers born into English don't think about these rules at
   all and violate them only when they are distracted or tired.

2. A few other rules—call them "the rules of Standard English"—distinguish the standard dialect from nonstandard
   ones: *He doesn't have any money* versus *He don't have no
   money*. Schooled writers observe these rules as naturally as
   they observe the Real Rules and think about them only

when they notice others violating them. The only writers who *self-consciously* follow them are those who were not born into Standard English and are striving to join the educated class.

3. Finally, some grammarians have invented a handful of rules that they think we all *should* observe—call them "Folklore." These are the rules that too many well-educated writers obsess over. Most date from the last half of the eighteenth century:

> Don't split infinitives, as in *to **quietly** leave.*
>
> Don't end a sentence with a preposition.

A few date from the twentieth century:

> Don't use *hopefully* for *I hope,* as in ***Hopefully,** it won't rain.*
>
> Don't use *which* for *that,* as in *a car **which** I sold.*

For 250 years, grammarians have accused the best writers of violating these invented rules, and for 250 years those writers have ignored them. Which is lucky for the grammarians, because if writers did obey all their rules, the grammarians would have to keep inventing new ones, or find another line of work. The fact is, none of these invented rules reflects the consensus of unself-conscious usage of our best writers.

In this lesson, we focus on this third kind of rule, the handful of invented ones, because only they vex those who already write Standard English.

Observing Rules Thoughtfully

It is, however, no simple matter to deal with these rules if you want to be thought of as someone who writes both clearly and "correctly." You could choose the worst-case policy: follow all the rules all the time because sometime, someone will criticize you for something—for beginning a sentence with *and* or ending it with *up.* But if you mindlessly obey all the rules all the time, you surrender a measure of choice. Worse, you risk becoming so obsessed with rules that you tie yourself in knots. And sooner or later, you will impose those rules—real or not—on others. After all, what good is learning a rule if all you can do is obey it?

The alternative to blind obedience is selective observance. But then you have to decide which rules to ignore. And then if you do ignore some rule, you may have to deal with those whose passionate memory for "good" grammar seems to endow them with the ability to see in a split infinitive a symptom of moral corruption and social decay.

If you want to avoid being accused of "lacking standards," but refuse to submit to whatever "rule" someone can dredge up from ninth-grade English, you have to know more about these invented rules than the rule-mongers do. The rest of this lesson helps you do that.

Two Kinds of Invented Rules

We can sort most of these invented rules into two groups: Folklore and Elegant Options.

1. *Folklore.* When you violate "rules" like these, few careful readers notice, much less care. So they are not rules at all, but folklore you can ignore (unless you are writing for someone with the power to demand even the folklore).

2. *Elegant Options.* When you ignore these rules, few readers notice. But paradoxically, some do when you observe them, because when you do, they detect signals of special care. So you can observe these rules or not, depending on how you want your readers to respond.

1. Folklore

These rules include those that most careful readers and writers ignore. You may not have heard of some of these "rules," but even if you have not yet had one inflicted on you, chances are that one day you will. In these examples, the quotations "violating" these rules are from writers of intellectual and scholarly stature or who, on matters of usage, are reliable conservatives (some are both). A check mark indicates those sentences that are acceptable Standard English, despite what some grammarians claim.

1. **"Don't begin sentences with *and* or *but*."** This passage ignores the "rule" twice:

   ✓ **But,** it will be asked, is tact not an individual gift, therefore highly variable in its choices? **And** if that is so, what guidance can a manual offer, other than that of its author's prejudices— mere impressionism?

   > —Wilson Follett, *Modern American Usage: A Guide,*
   > edited and completed by Jacques Barzun et al.

   On this matter, it's useful to consult the guide used by conservative writers: the *second* edition of H. W. Fowler's *A Dictionary of Modern English Usage* (first edition, Oxford University Press, 1926; second edition, 1965; third edition, 1997, considered too permissive by archconservatives). The second edition was edited by Sir Ernest Gowers, who, to Fowler's original entry for *and* in the first edition, added this:

   > That it is a solecism to begin a sentence with *and* is a faintly lingering superstition. (p. 29)

   To the original entry for *but,* he added "see *and.*" Some inexperienced writers do begin too many sentences with *and,* but that is an error not of grammar but of style.

   Some insecure writers also think they should not begin a sentence with *because.* Not this:

   ✓ **Because** we have access to so much historical fact, today we know a good deal about changes within the humanities which were not apparent to those of any age much before our own and which the individual scholar must constantly reflect on.

   —Walter Ong, S. J., "The Expanding Humanities and the Individual Scholar," *Publication of the Modern Language Association*

This folklore about *because* appears in no handbook, but it's gaining currency. It probably stems from advice aimed at avoiding sentence fragments like this one:

> The plan was rejected. **Because** it was incomplete.

2. **"Use the relative pronoun *that*—not *which*—for restrictive clauses."** Allegedly, not this:

> ✓ Next is a typical situation **which** a practiced writer corrects "for style" virtually by reflex action.
>
> —Jacques Barzun, *Simple and Direct* (p. 69)

Yet just a few sentences earlier, Barzun himself (one of our most eminent intellectual historians and critics of style) had asserted,

> Us[e] *that* with defining [i.e. restrictive] clauses except when stylistic reasons interpose.

(In the sentence in question, no such reasons interposed.)

A rule can have no force when someone as eminent as Barzun asserts it on one page and unself-consciously violates it on the next, and his "error" is never caught, not by his editors, not by his proofreaders, not even by Barzun himself.

This "rule" is relatively new. It first appeared in 1906 in Henry and Francis Fowler's *The King's English* (Oxford University Press; reprinted as an Oxford University Press paperback, 1973). The Fowlers thought that the random variation between *that* and *which* to begin a restrictive clause was messy, so they just asserted that writers should (with some exceptions) limit *which* to nonrestrictive clauses.

A nonrestrictive clause, you may recall, describes a noun that you can identify unambiguously without the information in that clause. For example,

✓ ABCO Inc. ended its bankruptcy, **which** it had filed in 1997.

A company can have only one bankruptcy at a time, so we can unambiguously identify the bankruptcy mentioned without the information in the clause. We therefore call that clause *nonrestrictive,* because it cannot "restrict" or narrow the meaning of the noun phrase *its bankruptcy* any more than it already is. We put a comma before the modifying clause and begin it with *which.* That rule is based on historical and contemporary usage.

But the Fowlers claimed that for *restrictive* clauses, we should use not *which* but only *that:* For example,

✓ ABCO Inc. sold a product **that** [*not **which**]* made millions.

Since ABCO presumably makes many products, the clause "restricts" the product to only the one that made millions, and so, said the Fowlers, it should begin with *that.*

Francis died in 1918, but Henry continued the family tradition with *A Dictionary of Modern English Usage.* In that landmark work, he discussed the finer points of *which* and *that,* then added this:

> Some there are who follow this principle now; but it would be idle to pretend that it is the practice either of most or of the best writers. (p. 635)

That wistful observation was kept in the second edition and again in the third. (For another *which,* see the passage by Walter Ong on p. 11.)

3. **"Use *fewer* with nouns you count, *less* with nouns you can't."** Allegedly not this:

   ✓ I can remember no **less** than five occasions when the correspondence columns of *The Times* rocked with volleys of letters . . .

   > —Noel Gilroy Annan, Lord Annan, "The Life of the Mind in British Universities Today," *American Council of Learned Societies Newsletter*

   No one uses *fewer* with mass nouns (*fewer sand*) but educated writers often use *less* with countable plural nouns (*less resources*).

4. **"Use *since* and *while* to refer only to time, not to mean *because* or *although.*"** Most careful writers use *since* with

a meaning close to *because* but with an added sense of "What follows I assume you already know":

✓ **Since** asbestos causes lung disease, avoid it.

Nor do most careful writers restrict *while* to its temporal sense (*We'll wait while you eat*), but also use it with a meaning close to "I assume you know what I state in this clause, but what I assert in the next will qualify it":

✓ **While** we agree on a date, we disagree about the place.

On the other hand, you might observe the advice to avoid *as* to signal causation, because it does so weakly:

As the expenses are minor, we need not discuss them.

Use *since*.

Here's the point: If writers we judge competent regularly violate some alleged rule, then the rule can have no force. In those cases, it's not writers who should change their usage but grammarians who should change their rules.

---

2. Elegant Options

These next "rules" complement the Real Rules: call them *Elegant Options*. Most readers do not notice when you observe a Real Rule, but do when violates you it (like that). On the other hand, few readers notice when you violate one of these optional rules, but some do when you observe it, because doing so adds a note of formality.

1. **"Don't split infinitives."** Purists condemn Dwight MacDonald, a linguistic archconservative, for this sentence (my emphasis in all the examples that follow).

✓ One wonders why Dr. Gove and his editors did not think of labeling *knowed* as substandard right where it occurs, and one suspects that they wanted **to slightly conceal** the fact . . .

—"The String Untuned," *The New Yorker*

They would require

. . . they wanted **to conceal slightly** the fact . . .

Infinitives are now split so commonly that when you avoid splitting one, careful readers may think you are trying to be especially correct, whether you are or not.

2. **"Use *whom* as the OBJECT of a verb or preposition."** Purists would condemn William Zinsser for this use of *who:*

✓ Soon after you confront this matter of preserving your identity, another question will occur to you: "**Who** am I writing for?"

—*On Writing Well*

They would insist on

. . . another question will occur to you: "For **whom** am I writing?"

Most readers take *whom* as a sign of self-conscious correctness, so when a writer uses it incorrectly, that choice is probably a sign of insecurity, as in this sentence:

The committee must decide **whom** should be promoted.

In that sentence, *whom* is the subject of the verb *should be promoted,* so it should be *who.* Here is an actual rule: Use *who* when it's the subject of a verb *in its own clause;* use *whom* only when it's an object in its own clause.

3. **"Don't end a sentence with a preposition."** Purists would condemn Sir Ernest Gowers, editor of Fowler's second edition, for this:

✓ The peculiarities of legal English are often used as a stick to beat the official **with.**

—*The Complete Plain Words*

and insist on this:

> . . . a stick **with which** to beat the official.

The first is correct; the second more formal. (Again, see the Ong passage on p. 11.) And when you choose to shift both the preposition and its *whom* to the left, that sentence seems even more formal. Compare:

✓ The man I met with was the man I had written **to.**

✓ The man **with whom** I met was the man **to whom** I had written.

A final preposition can, however, end a sentence weakly (see pp. 112–113). George Orwell may have chosen to end this next sentence with *from* to make a sly point about English grammar, but I suspect it just landed there (and note the "incorrect" *which* six words from the end):

> [The defense of the English language] has nothing to do with . . . the setting up of a "standard English" **which** must never be departed **from.**
>
> —George Orwell, "Politics and the English Language"

This would have been less awkward and more emphatic:

> We do not defend English just to create a "standard English" whose rules we must always obey.

4. **"Use the singular with *none* and *any*."** Historically *none* and *any* were originally singular, but today most writers use them as plurals. Therefore, if you use them as singular, some readers will notice. The second is a bit more formal than the first:

✓ **None** of the reasons **are** sufficient to end the project.

✓ **None** of the reasons **is** sufficient to end the project.

When you are under the closest scrutiny, you might choose to observe these optional rules. Ordinarily, though, they are ignored by most careful writers, which is to say they are not rules at all, but rather stylistic choices to signal a bit of formality. If you adopt the worst-case approach and observe them all, all the time—well, private virtues are their own reward.

Hobgoblins

For some reason, a handful of items has become the object of particularly zealous abuse. There's no explaining why; none of them interferes with clarity or concision.

1. **"Never use *like* for *as* or *as if*."** Not this:

   > These operations failed **like** the earlier ones did.

   But this:

   > These operations failed **as** the earlier ones did.

   Like became a subordinating conjunction in the eighteenth century when writers began to drop *as* from the phrase *like as*, leaving *like* as the conjunction. This process is called *elision* and is a common linguistic change. It is telling that the editor of the second edition of Fowler (the one favored by conservatives) deleted *like* for *as* from Fowler's list of "Illiteracies" and moved it into the category of "Sturdy Indefensibles."

2. **"Don't use *hopefully* to mean 'I hope.'"** Not this:

   > ✓ Hopefully, it will not rain.

   But this:

   > ✓ It is hoped that it will not rain.

   This "rule" dates from the twentieth century; it has no basis in logic or grammar. It parallels the usage of other words that no one abuses, words such as *candidly, frankly, sadly,* and *happily:*

   - ✓ Candidly, we may fail. (That is, *I am candid when I say we may fail*.)
   - ✓ Seriously, we must go. (That is, *I am serious when I say we must go*.)

3. **"Don't use *finalize* to mean 'finish' or 'complete.'"** But *finalize* doesn't mean just "finish." It means "to clean up the last few details," a sense captured by no other word. Moreover, if we think *finalize* is bad because *-ize* is ugly, we would have to reject *nationalize, synthesize,* and *rationalize,* along with hundreds of other useful words.

4. **"Don't use *impact* as a verb, as in *The survey* impacted *our strategy.* Use it only as a noun, as in *The survey had* an impact *on our strategy.*"** *Impact* has been used as a verb since the seventeenth century, but on some people, historical evidence has none.

5. **"Don't modify absolute words such as *perfect, unique, final,* or *complete* with *very, more, quite,* and so on."** That rule would have ruled out this familiar sentence:

   ✓ We the People of the United States, in order to form a **more perfect** union . . .

   (Even so, this is a rule worth following most of the time.)

6. **"Never ever use *irregardless* for *regardless* or *irrespective.*"** However arbitrary this rule is, it's one you should follow.

Some Words That Attract Special Attention

A few words are so often confused with others that careful readers are likely to note your care when you correctly distinguish them—*flaunt* and *flout* for example. When you use them correctly, those who think the difference matters are likely to note that at least *you* know that *flaunt* means "to display conspicuously" and that *flout* means "to scorn a rule or standard." Thus if you chose to scorn the rule about *flaunt* and *flout,* you would not flout your flaunting it, but flaunt your flouting it. Here are some others:

   aggravate means "to make worse." It does not mean to **annoy.** You can aggravate an injury but not a person.

anticipate means "to prepare for a contingency." It does not mean just **expect.** You anticipate a question when you prepare its answer before it's asked; if you know it's coming but don't prepare, you only expect it.

anxious means "uneasy," not **eager.** You're eager to leave if you're happy to. You're anxious about leaving if it makes you nervous.

blackmail means "to extort by threatening to reveal damaging information." It does not mean simply **coerce.** One country cannot blackmail another with nuclear weapons when it only threatens to use them.

cohort means "a group who attends on someone." It does not mean a single accompanying person. If Prince Charles marries his friend she will become his **consort;** his hangers-on will still be his *cohort.*

comprise means "to include all parts in a single unit." It does not mean **constitute.** The alphabet is not comprised by its letters; it comprises them. Letters constitute the alphabet; it is constituted by them.

continuous means "without interruption." It is not synonymous with **continual,** which means an activity through time, with interruptions. If you continuously interrupt someone, that person will never say a word because your interruption will never stop. If you continually interrupt, you let the other person finish a sentence from time to time.

disinterested means "neutral." It does not mean **uninterested.** A judge should be disinterested in the outcome of a case, but not uninterested in it. (Incidentally, the original meaning of *disinterested* was "to be uninterested.")

enormity means "hugely bad." It does not mean **enormous.** In private, a belch might be enormous, but at a state funeral, it would also be an enormity.

fortuitous means "by chance." It does not mean **fortunate.** You are fortunate when you fortuitously pick the right number in the lottery.

> ***fulsome*** means "sickeningly excessive." It does not mean just "much." All of us enjoy full praise, except when it becomes fulsome.

> ***notorious*** means "well known for bad behavior." It does not mean **famous.** Frank Sinatra was a famous singer but a notorious bully.

These days only a few readers care about these distinctions, but they may be just those whose judgment carries special weight when it matters most. It takes only a few minutes to learn to use these words in ways that testify to your precision, so it may be worth doing so, especially if you also think their distinctions are worth preserving.

On the other hand, you get no points for correctly distinguishing *imply* and *infer, principal* and *principle, accept* and *except, capital* and *capitol, affect* and *effect, proceed* and *precede, discrete* and *discreet.* That's just expected of schooled writers. Most careful readers also notice when a Latinate or Greek plural noun is used as a singular, so you might want to keep these straight, too:

Singular	datum	criterion	medium	stratum	phenomenon
Plural	data	criteria	media	strata	phenomena

A SPECIAL PROBLEM: PRONOUNS AND GENDER BIAS

We expect literate writers to make verbs agree with subjects:

> ✓ Our **reasons** ARE based on solid evidence.

We also expect their pronouns to agree with antecedents. Not this:

> Early **efforts** to oppose the hydrogen bomb failed because **it** ignored political issues. **No one** wanted to expose **themselves** to anti-Communist hysteria.

But this:

> ✓ Early **efforts** to oppose the hydrogen bomb failed because **they** ignored political issues. **No one** wanted to expose **himself** to anti-Communist hysteria.

There are, however, two problems.

First, do we use a singular or plural pronoun when referring to a noun that is singular in grammar but plural in meaning? For example, when we refer to a *group, committee, staff, administration,* and so on, do we use *it* or *they?* And do we use a singular or plural verb? Some writers use a singular verb and pronoun when the group acts as a single entity:

> ✓ The **committee has** met but has not yet made **its** decision.

But they use a plural verb and pronoun when its members act individually:

> ✓ The **faculty have** the memo, but not all of **them** have read it.

These days plurals are irregularly used in both senses (but the plural is the rule in British English).

Second, what pronoun do we use to refer to *someone, everyone, no one* and to singular nouns that signal no gender: *teacher, doctor, student?* We casually use *they:*

> **Everyone** knows **they** must answer for **their** actions.
>
> When **a person** is on drugs, it is hard to help **them.**

More formal usage requires a singular pronoun:

> ✓ **Everyone** realizes that **he** must answer for **his actions.**

But the formal rule raises the problem of biased language.

Common sense demands that we not gratuitously offend readers, but if we reject *he* as a generic pronoun because it's biased and *they* because some readers consider it ungrammatical, we are left with a lot of bad choices. Some writers choose a clumsy *he or she;* others choose a worse *he/she* or even *s/he.*

If **a writer** ignores the ethnicity of **his or her** readers, **s/he** may respond in ways **the writer** would not expect to words that to **him or her** are innocent of bias.

Some writers substitute plurals for singulars:

✓ When **writers** ignore **their** readers' ethnicity, **they** may respond in **ways they** might not expect to **words** that are to **them** innocent of bias.

But in that sentence, *they, their,* and *them* are confusing, because they can refer to two different referents, and to the careful ear, a sentence with singular nouns and pronouns seems a shade more precise than one with plural nouns and pronouns. Compare the sentence above with this one:

If **a writer** ignores the ethnicity of **his reader, his reader** might respond to **a word** in **a way** that **the writer** would not expect.

We can try a first person *we,*

✓ If **we** ignore the ethnicity of **our** readers, they may respond in ways **we** would not expect to words that to **us** are innocent of bias.

But *we* can also be ambiguous. We could also try impersonal abstraction, but that creates its own problem:

Failure to consider ethnicity may lead to an unexpected response to words considered innocent of bias.

Finally, we can alternately use *he* and *she,* as I have. But that's not a perfect solution, because some readers find a *she* as intrusive as *he/she.* A reviewer in the *New York Times,* for example, wondered what to make of an author whom the reviewer charged with attempting to

right history's wrongs to women by referring to random examples as "she," as in "Ask a particle physicist what happens when a quark is knocked out of a proton, and she will tell you . . . ," which strikes this reader as oddly patronizing to women.

(We might wonder how it strikes women particle physicists.)

For years to come, we will have a problem with singular generic pronouns, and to some readers, any solution will be awkward. I suspect that eventually we will accept the plural *they* as a correct singular:

✓ **No one** should turn in **their** writing unedited.

Some claim that in such compromises we cave in to lazy imprecision. Whatever the future holds, we have a choice now, and that's not entirely a bad thing, because our choices define who we are.

I suspect that those who observe all the rules all the time do so not because they want to protect the integrity of the language or the quality of our culture, but because they want to assert a style of their own. Some of us are straightforward and plain speaking; others take pleasure in a bit of elegance, in a touch of fastidiously self-conscious "class." It is an impulse we should not scorn, so long as it's not a pretext for discrimination, and includes a concern for the more important matters to which we now turn—the choices that define not "good grammar," but clarity and grace.

3

Actions

*Everything that can be thought at all
can be thought clearly.
Everything that can be said can be said clearly.*
—LUDWIG WITTGENSTEIN

MAKING JUDGMENTS

We have words enough to praise writing we like: *clear, direct, concise,* and more than enough to abuse writing we don't: *unclear, indirect, abstract, dense, complex.* We could use those words to distinguish these two sentences:

1a. The cause of our schools' failure at teaching basic skills is not understanding the influence of cultural background on learning.

1b. Our schools have failed to teach basic skills because they do not understand how cultural backgrounds influence the way children learn.

Most of us would call (1a) a bit complex, (1b) clearer and more direct. But those words don't refer to anything *in* either sentence; they describe how those sentences make us *feel.* When we say that (1a) is *unclear,* we mean that *we* had a hard time understanding it; when we say it is *dense,* we mean that *we* struggled through it.

The real problem is to understand what it is about those two sentences that makes us feel as we do. Only then can you predict when your readers will think your sentences are dense and unclear so that you can revise them. To do that, you have to understand what counts as a well-told story.

TELLING STORIES ABOUT CHARACTERS AND THEIR ACTIONS

It is easy to state the general principle of clarity: match the important actions in your sentences to verbs, and make the characters in your story their subjects.

Here's a story with a problem:

> 2a. Once upon a time, as a walk through the woods was taking place on the part of Little Red Riding Hood, the Wolf's jump out from behind a tree occurred, causing her fright.

We prefer something closer to this:

> ✓ 2b. Once upon a time, Little Red Riding Hood was walking through the woods, when the Wolf jumped out from behind a tree and frightened her.

Most readers think (2b) tells its story more clearly than (2a), because it follows those two principles I stated:

- In (2a), the sentence that seems less clear, the characters are not subjects and their actions are not verbs.
- In (2b), the sentence that seems clearer, the characters are subjects and their actions are verbs.

Those two principles seem simple enough, but they need some explanation. (To get the most out of this lesson and the next, you should be able to identify verbs, simple subjects, and whole subjects.)

Principle of Clarity 1: Make Main Characters Subjects

Look at the subjects in (2a). The simple subjects (boldfaced) and main characters (italicized) are different words:

2a. Once upon a time, as a **walk** through the woods was taking place on the part of *Little Red Riding Hood*, *the Wolf's* **jump** out from behind a tree occurred, causing *her* fright.

Subjects are not characters; they are actions expressed as abstract NOUNS, *walk* and *jump:*

SUBJECT	VERB
a **walk** through the woods	was taking place
the *Wolf's* **jump** out from behind a tree	occurred

The whole subject of *occurred* has a character *in* it: *the **Wolf's** jump*, but *the Wolf* is only attached to the simple subject *jump;* it is not *the* subject.

   Contrast those abstract subjects with the short, specific subjects (boldfaced) in (2b).

2b. Once upon a time, ***Little Red Riding Hood*** was walking through the woods, when ***the Wolf*** jumped out from behind a tree and frightened her.

The subjects and the main characters are now the same words:

SUBJECT/CHARACTER	VERB
Little Red Riding Hood	was walking
the Wolf	jumped

Principle of Clarity 2:
Make Important Actions Verbs

Now look at how the actions and verbs differ. In (2a), the actions are not verbs but abstract nouns (actions are boldfaced; verbs are capitalized):

2a. Once upon a time, as a **walk** through the woods WAS TAKING place on the part of Little Red Riding Hood, the Wolf's **jump** out from behind a tree OCCURRED, causing her **fright**.

And note the vague verbs: *was taking, occurred.*

In (2b), the clearer sentence, the verbs are specific because the actions and verbs are the same words:

✓ 2b. Once upon a time, Little Red Riding Hood **WAS WALKING** through the woods, when the Wolf **JUMPED** out from behind a tree and **FRIGHTENED** her.

Here's the point: In the sentence that seems wordy and indirect, its two main characters, Little Red Riding Hood and the Wolf, are *not* subjects, and their actions—*walk, jump,* and *fright*—are *not* verbs. In the more direct version, (2b), those two main characters *are* subjects and their main actions *are* verbs. In short, in (2a), the story and the grammar of the sentence don't match; in (2b), they do. That's why we prefer (2b).

FAIRY TALES AND ACADEMIC WRITING

Fairy tales may seem a long way from writing in college or on the job, but even there, sentences tell stories. Compare these two:

3a. The Federalists' argument in regard to the destabilization of government by popular democracy was based on their belief in the tendency of factions to further their self-interest at the expense of the common good.

✓ 3b. The Federalists argued that popular democracy destabilized government, because they believed that factions tended to further their self-interest at the expense of the common good.

We can analyze those two sentences as we did the ones about Little Red Riding Hood.

Sentence (3a) feels dense for two reasons. First, its characters and subjects are different words. The simple subject is *argument,* but the main characters are *Federalists, popular democracy*, and *factions* (the characters are italicized; the simple subject is boldfaced):

3a. *The Federalists'* **argument** in regard to the destabilization of *government* by *popular democracy* was based on *their* belief in the tendency of *factions* to further *their* self-interest at the expense of the common good.

Second, most of the actions (boldfaced) are not verbs (capitalized), but rather abstract nouns (also boldfaced):

3a. The Federalists' **argument** in regard to the **destabilization** of government by popular democracy WAS BASED on their **belief** in the **tendency** of factions to FURTHER their self-interest at the expense of the common good.

Notice in particular how long the whole subject of (3a) is and how little meaning is expressed by its main verb *was based:*

WHOLE SUBJECT	VERB
The Federalists' argument in regard to the destabilization of government by popular democracy	was based

Readers think (3b) is clearer, first because its characters (italicized) *are* subjects (boldfaced):

3b. The ***Federalists*** argued that ***popular democracy*** destabilized government, because ***they*** believed that ***factions*** tended to further *their* self-interest at the expense of the common good.

And second, all the actions (boldfaced) are verbs (capitalized):

3b. The Federalists ARGUED that popular democracy DESTABILIZED government, because they BELIEVED that factions TENDED to FURTHER their self-interest at the expense of the common good.

Note that all those subjects are short and specific and that the verbs express specific actions:

WHOLE SUBJECT/CHARACTER	VERB/ACTION
the Federalists	argued
popular democracy	destabilized
they	believed
factions	tended to further

In the rest of this lesson, we look at actions and verbs; in the next, at characters and subjects.

Verbs and Actions

Our principle is this: *A sentence seems clear when its important actions are in verbs.* Look at how sentences (4a) and (4b) express their actions. In (4a), actions (boldfaced) are not verbs (capitalized); they are nouns:

> 4a. Our **lack** of data PREVENTED **evaluation** of UN **actions** in **targeting** funds to areas most in **need** of **assistance.**

In (4b), on the other hand, the actions are almost all verbs:

> ✓ 4b. Because we LACKED data, we could not EVALUATE whether the UN had TARGETED funds to areas that most NEEDED **assistance.**

Readers will think your writing is dense if you use lots of abstract nouns, especially ones derived from verbs and adjectives, nouns ending in *-tion, -ment, -ence,* and so on, *especially when those nouns are subjects of verbs.*

Such nouns have a technical name: *nominalization.* The word illustrates its own meaning: When we nominalize *nominalize,* we create the nominalization *nominalization.* Here are a few examples:

VERB → NOMINALIZATION			ADJECTIVE → NOMINALIZATION		
discover	→	discovery	careless	→	carelessness
resist	→	resistance	different	→	difference
react	→	reaction	proficient	→	proficiency

We can also nominalize a verb by adding *-ing* (making it a gerund):

> She flies → her flying   We sang → our singing

Some nominalizations and verbs are identical:

> hope → hope   result → result   repair → repair

We **REQUEST** that you **REVIEW** the data.

Our **request** IS that you DO a **review** of the data.

(Some actions can also hide in adjectives: *It is applicable → it applies.* Some others: *indicative, dubious, argumentative, deserving.*)

No feature of style more characterizes abstract, indirect, difficult academic and professional writing than lots of nominalizations, especially when they are subjects of verbs.

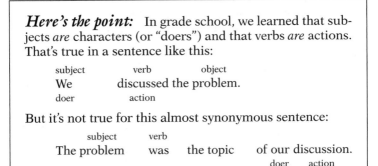

Here's the point: In grade school, we learned that subjects *are* characters (or "doers") and that verbs *are* actions. That's true in a sentence like this:

      subject   verb   object
      We   discussed the problem.
      doer   action

But it's not true for this almost synonymous sentence:

       subject   verb
      The problem   was   the topic   of our discussion.
                                          doer   action

We can move characters and actions almost wherever we want in a sentence, and subjects and verbs don't have to be any particular thing at all. But readers prefer that most subjects be characters and most verbs be actions. When you match them up in most of your sentences, your readers are likely to think your prose is clear and direct.

DIAGNOSIS AND REVISION

You can use the principles to explain why your readers will judge your prose as they do. But more important, you can also use them to identify sentences that your readers would want you to revise, and then to revise them. Revising is a three-step process: diagnose, analyze, revise.

1. **Diagnose.** To predict how a reader will judge your style, do this:
   a. Ignoring short (four- or five-word) introductory phrases, underline the first seven or eight words in each sentence.
   b. Look for two things:
      - You have underlined abstract nouns as simple subjects.
      - You read at least six or seven words before you get to a verb.
2. **Analyze.** If you find such sentences, do this:
   a. Decide who your main characters are, particularly flesh-and-blood characters (more about this in the next lesson).
   b. Look for the actions that those characters perform, especially in nominalizations, those abstract nouns derived from verbs.
3. **Revise.**
   a. If the actions are in nominalizations, change them into verbs.
   b. Make the characters the subjects of those verbs.
   c. Rewrite the sentence with conjunctions like *because, if, when, although, why, how, whether,* or *that*.

For example, let's diagnose and revise this sentence:

The outsourcing of high-tech work to Asia by corporations means the loss of jobs for many American workers.

Diagnose: Underline the first seven or eight words:

<u>The outsourcing of high-tech work to Asia</u> by corporations means the loss of jobs for many American workers.

We do not see a character *as* a subject or a verb expressing an important action.

Analyze: Who are the characters and what are their actions?

Characters: *American workers, corporations*
Actions: *outsourcing, loss*

Revise: Turn the actions into verbs and make the characters their subjects:

> *Many American workers* **are losing** their jobs, because *corporations are outsourcing* high-tech work to Asia.

Some Common Patterns

You can quickly spot and revise three common patterns of nominalizations.

1. **The nominalization is the subject of an empty verb:**

   > The **intention** of the committee IS to audit the records.

   a. Change the nominalization to a verb:

   > intention → intend

   b. Identify the character that would be the subject of that verb:

   > The intention of **the committee** is to audit the records.

   c. Make that character the subject of the verb:

   > *The committee* **INTENDS** to audit the records.

2. **A nominalization follows *there is* or *there are:***

   > There IS no **need** for *our* further **study** of this problem.

   a. Change the nominalization to a verb:

   > need → need   study → study

   b. Identify the character that should be the subject of the verb:

   > There is no need for **our** further study of this problem.

   c. Make that character the subject of the verb:

   > no need → we need   our study → we study

   > *We* **NEED** not **STUDY** this problem further.

3. **One nominalization is a subject and a second appears after an empty verb like *be, seems, has,* etc.:**

   Our **loss** in sales WAS a result of their **expansion** of outlets.

   a. Revise the nominalizations into verbs:

   loss → lose   expansion → expand

   b. Identify the characters that would be the subjects of those verbs:

   Our loss in sales was a result of **their** expansion of outlets.

   c. Make those characters subjects of those verbs:

   we lose   they expand

   d. Link the new clauses with a logical connection:

   - To express simple cause: *because, since, when*
   - To express conditional cause: *if, provided that, so long as*
   - To contradict expected causes: *though, although, unless*

Our **loss** in sales	→	*We* **LOST** sales
was the result of	→	**because**
their **expansion** of outlets	→	*they* **EXPANDED** outlets

   Two other patterns invite you to look for nominalizations after verbs. In these cases, the subject is often a character.

4. **A nominalization follows an empty verb:**

   The *agency* CONDUCTED an **investigation** into the matter.

   a. Change the nominalization to a verb:

   investigation → investigate

   b. Replace the empty verb with the new verb:

   conducted → investigated

   ✓ The *agency* INVESTIGATED the matter.

5. **Two or three nominalizations in a row are joined by prepositions:**

> We did a **review** of the **evolution** of the brain.

a. Turn the first nominalization into a verb:

> review → review

b. Either leave the second nominalization as it is or turn it into a verb in a clause beginning with *how* or *why:*

> evolution of the brain → how the brain evolved

> First, *we* REVIEWED the **evolution** of the *brain.*

> ✓ First, *we* REVIEWED how *the brain* EVOLVED.

Some Happy Consequences

When you consistently rely on verbs to express key actions, your readers benefit in many ways:

1. Your sentences are likely to be more concrete, because they will have concrete subjects and verbs. Compare:

> There WAS an affirmative **decision** for **expansion.**

> ✓ *The Director* DECIDED to EXPAND the program.

2. Your sentences are more concise. When you use nominalizations, you have to use articles like *a* and *the* and prepositions such as *of, by,* and *in.* You don't need them when you use verbs and conjunctions (italicized):

> A **revision** *of* the program WILL RESULT *in* **increases** *in* our **efficiency** *in the* **servicing** *of* clients.

> ✓ *If* we REVISE the program, we CAN SERVE clients more EFFICIENTLY.

3. The logic of your sentences is clearer. When you nominalize verbs, you link actions with fuzzy prepositions and phrases such as *of, by,* and *on the part of.* But when you use verbs,

you can link clauses with precise SUBORDINATING CONJUNC-
TIONS such as *because, although,* and *if:*

> Our more effective presentation of our study resulted in our
> success, despite an earlier start by others.

> ✓ **Although** others started earlier, we succeeded **because** we pre-
> sented our study more effectively.

4. Your sentences tell a more coherent story. This next sequence of actions distorts their chronology. (The numbers
   refer to the real sequence of events.)

> Decisions[4] in regard to administration[5] of medication despite
> inability[2] of an irrational patient appearing[1] in a Trauma Cen-
> ter to provide legal consent[3] rest with the attending physician
> alone.

When we revise those actions into verbs and reorder them,
we get a more coherent narrative:

> ✓ When a patient appears[1] in a Trauma Center and behaves[2] so
> irrationally that he cannot legally consent[3] to treatment, only
> the attending physician can decide[4] whether to medicate[5] him.

A Qualification: Useful Nominalizations

I have so relentlessly urged you to turn nominalizations into
verbs that you might think you should never use one. But in
fact, you can't write well without them. The trick is to know
which to keep and which to turn into verbs. Keep these:

1. A nominalization as a short subject refers to a previous sentence:

> ✓ **These arguments** all depend on a single unproven claim.

> ✓ **This decision** can lead to positive outcomes.

Those nominalizations link one sentence to another in a cohesive flow.

2. A short nominalization replaces an awkward *The fact that:*

   The fact that she ACKNOWLEDGED the problem impressed me.

   ✓ Her **acknowledgment** of the problem impressed me.

   But then, why not this:

   ✓ *She* IMPRESSED me when *she* ACKNOWLEDGED the problem.

3. A nominalization names what would be the object of the verb:

   I accepted *what she* REQUESTED.

   ✓ I accepted her **request.**

   This kind of nominalization feels more concrete than an abstract one. However, contrast *request* above with this next sentence, where *request* is more of an action:

   Her **request** for **assistance** CAME after the deadline.

   ✓ She REQUESTED **assistance** after the deadline.

4. A nominalization refers to a concept so familiar to your readers that to them, it is a character (more about this in the next lesson):

   ✓ Few problems have so divided us as **abortion** on **demand.**

   ✓ The Equal Rights **Amendment** was an issue in past **elections.**

   ✓ **Taxation** without **representation** did not spark the American **Revolution.**

4

Characters

When character is lost, all is lost.
—ANONYMOUS

UNDERSTANDING THE IMPORTANCE OF CHARACTERS

Readers judge writing to be clear and direct when they see crucial actions in verbs. Compare (1a) with (1b):

1a. The CIA feared the president would recommend to Congress that it reduce its budget.

1b. The CIA had fears that the president would send a recommendation to Congress that it make a reduction in its budget.

But while sentence (1a) is a third shorter than (1b), some readers don't sense a big difference in their clarity.

But now compare (1b) and (1c):

1b. The CIA had fears that the president would send a recommendation to Congress that it make a reduction in its budget.

1c. The fear of the CIA was that a recommendation from the president to Congress would be for a reduction in its budget.

Every reader thinks that (1c) is much less clear than either (1a) or (1b).

The reason is this: In both (1a) and (1b), important characters are short, specific subjects of verbs:

1a. **The CIA** FEARED **the president** would RECOMMEND to Congress that **it** REDUCE its budget.

1b. **The CIA** HAD fears that **the president** would SEND a recommendation to Congress that **it** MAKE a reduction in its budget.

But the two subjects in (1c) are not specific characters, but abstractions.

1c. **The fear of the CIA** WAS **that a recommendation from the president to Congress** WOULD BE for a reduction in its budget.

The main characters (the CIA, the president, and Congress) are not subjects, but objects of prepositions:

1c. The fear *of* **the CIA** was that a recommendation *from* **the president** *to* **Congress** would be for a reduction in its budget.

The different verbs in (1a) and (1b) make some difference, but the different subjects in (1c) make a bigger difference.

Here's the point: Readers want actions in verbs, but even more they want characters as their subjects. We give readers a big problem when for no good reason we do not name characters in subjects, or worse, delete them entirely, like this:

1d. There was fear that there would be a recommendation for a budget reduction.

Who fears? Who recommends? Who reduces? It is important to express actions in verbs, but the *first* principle of a clear style is this: Make the subjects of most of your verbs short, specific, and concrete.

DIAGNOSIS AND REVISION

Finding and Relocating Characters

To get characters into subjects, you have to know three things:

1. when you haven't done that
2. if you haven't, where you should look for characters
3. what you should do when you find them (or don't)

For example, this sentence feels indirect and impersonal.

> Governmental intervention in fast changing technologies has led to the distortion of market evolution and interference in new product development.

Let's diagnose that sentence:

1. **Skim the first seven or eight words:**

   > <u>Governmental intervention in fast changing technologies has led</u> to the distortion of market evolution and interference in new product development.

   In those first few words, readers want to see characters as the subjects of verbs. But in that example, they don't.

2. **Find the main characters.** They may be possessive pronouns attached to nominalizations, objects of prepositions, particularly *by* and *of*, or only implied. In that sentence about governmental intervention, one main character is in the adjective *governmental;* the other is in the object of a preposition: *of market evolution.*

3. **Skim the passage for actions involving those characters, particularly actions buried in nominalizations; then make them verbs and the relevant characters their subjects.** The question to ask is "Who's doing what?"

governmental **intervention**	→	*government* **intervenes**
distortion	→	*[government]* **distorts**
market **evolution**	→	*markets* **evolve**

interference	→	*[government]* **interferes**
development	→	*[market]* **develops**

Now reassemble those new subjects and verbs into a sentence, using conjunctions such as *if, although, because, when, how,* and *why:*

✓ **When** a *government* **INTERVENES** in fast changing technologies, *it* **DISTORTS** how *markets* **EVOLVE** or **INTERFERES** with their ability to **DEVELOP** new products.

Be aware that just as actions can be in adjectives (*reliable* → *rely*), so can characters:

Medieval *theological* debates often addressed issues considered trivial by modern *philosophical* thought.

When you find a character implied in an adjective, revise in the same way:

✓ *Medieval theologians* often debated issues that *modern philosophers* consider trivial.

Here's the point: The first step in diagnosing your style is to look at your subjects. If you do not see your main characters there, your next step is to look for them. They can be in objects of prepositions, in possessive pronouns, or in adjectives. Once you find them, look for actions they are involved in. Then make those characters the subjects of verbs naming their actions.

Reconstructing Absent Characters

Readers have the biggest problem with sentences devoid of *all* characters:

A decision was made in favor of doing a study of the disagreements.

That sentence could mean either of these, and more:

> We decided that I should study why they disagreed.
>
> I decided that you should study why he disagreed.

The writer may know who is doing what, but readers might not and so usually need help.

Sometimes we omit characters to make a general statement.

> Research strategies that look for more than one variable are of more use in understanding factors in psychiatric disorder than strategies based on the assumption that the presence of psychopathology is dependent on a single gene or on strategies in which only one biological variable is studied.

But when we try to revise that into something clearer, we have to invent characters, then decide what to call them. Do we use *one* or *we,* or name a generic "doer"?

> ✓ If *one/we/researchers* are to understand what causes psychiatric disorder, *one/we/they* should use research strategies that look for more than one variable rather than assume that a single gene is responsible for psychopathology or adopt a strategy in which *one/we/they* study only one biological variable.

To most of us, *one* feels stiff, but *we* may be ambiguous because it can refer just to the writer, or to the writer and others but not the reader, or to the reader and writer but not others, or to everyone.

But if you avoid both nominalizations and vague pronouns, you can slide into passive verbs (I'll discuss them in a moment):

> To understand what makes patients vulnerable to psychiatric disorders, strategies that look for more than one variable SHOULD BE USED rather than strategies in which it IS ASSUMED that a gene causes psychopathology or only one biological variable IS STUDIED.

In some cases, characters are so remote that you just have to start over:

> There are good reasons that account for the lack of evidence.
>
> ✓ I can explain why I have not found any evidence.

Abstractions as Characters

So far, I've discussed characters as if they had to be flesh-and-blood people. But you can tell stories whose main characters are abstractions, including nominalizations, so long as you make them the subjects of a series of sentences that tell a coherent story. Here's a story about a character called "freedom of speech," two nominalizations.

> ✓ No right is more fundamental to a free society than **freedom of speech. Free speech** served the left in the 1960s when it protested the Vietnam War, and **it** is now used by the right when it claims that speech includes political contributions. **The doctrine of free speech** has been embraced by all sides to protect themselves against those who would silence unpopular views. As a legal concept, **it** arose . . .

The phrase *freedom of speech* (or its equivalents *free speech* and *it*) is a virtual character because it's the subject of a series of sentences and involved in actions such as *served, is used, has been embraced,* and *arose.* Free speech is the central character in the story told by that paragraph.

But when you do use abstractions as characters, you can create a problem. A story about an abstraction as familiar as *free speech* is clear enough, but if you surround an abstract character with a lot of other abstractions, readers may feel that your writing is dense and complex.

For example, few of us are familiar with the concepts of "prospective and immediate intention," so most of us are likely to struggle with a story about them, especially when that word *intention* is surrounded by lots of other abstractions (actions are boldfaced; human characters are italicized):

> The **argument** is this. The cognitive component of **intention** exhibits a high degree of **complexity**. **Intention** is temporally divisible into two: prospective **intention** and immediate **intention**. The cognitive function of prospective **intention** is the **representation** of a *subject*'s similar past **actions**, *his* current situation, and *his* course of future **actions**. That is, the cognitive component of prospective **intention** is a **plan**. The cognitive func-

tion of immediate **intention** is the **monitoring** and **guidance** of ongoing bodily **movement**.

—Myles Brand, *Intending and Acting*

We can make that passage clearer if we tell it from the point of view of flesh-and-blood characters (they are italicized; "denominalized" verbs are boldfaced and capitalized):

✓ *I* **ARGUE** this about intention. It has a complex cognitive component of two temporal kinds: prospective intention and immediate intention. *We* use prospective intention to **REPRESENT** how *we* have **ACTED** in our past and present and how *we* will **ACT** in the future. That is, *we* use the cognitive component of prospective intention to help *us* **PLAN**. *We* use immediate intention to **MONITOR** and **GUIDE** *our* bodies as *we* **MOVE** them.

But have I made this passage say something that the writer didn't mean? Some argue that any change in form changes meaning. In this case, the writer might offer an opinion, but only his readers could decide whether the two passages have different meanings, because at the end of the day, a passage means only what careful readers think it does.

Here's the point: Most readers want the subjects of verbs to name the main characters in a story, and those main characters to be flesh-and-blood. But often, you must write about abstract concepts. If you do, then turn them into virtual characters by making them the subjects of verbs that tell a story. If readers are familiar with your abstractions, no problem. But when they are not, avoid using lots of other abstract nominalizations around them. When you revise an abstract passage, you may have a problem if the hidden characters are "people in general." You can try *we* or a general term for whoever is doing the action, such as *researchers, social critics, one,* and so on. But the fact is, the English language has no good solution for this problem—that of naming a generic "doer."

Characters and Passive Verbs

More than any other advice, you probably remember "Write in the active voice, not in the passive." That's not bad advice, but it has exceptions.

When you write in the active voice, you typically put

- a character as the agent of an action in the subject
- the goal or receiver of an action in a direct object:

	subject	verb	object
Active:	I	lost	the money.
	character/agent	action	goal

The passive differs in three ways:

1. The subject names the goal of the action.
2. A form of *be* precedes a verb in its past participle form.
3. The agent of the action is in a *by*-phrase or dropped entirely:

	subject	be + verb	prepositional phrase
Passive:	The money	was lost	[by me].
	goal	action	character/agent

The terms *active* and *passive*, however, are ambiguous, because they can refer not only to those two grammatical constructions but also to how a sentence makes us *feel*. We call a sentence passive if it feels flat, regardless of whether its verb is actually in the passive voice. For example, compare these two sentences.

We will succeed if we can effectively control costs.

Success will depend on cost control effectiveness.

Grammatically, both sentences are in the active voice, but the second *feels* passive, for three reasons:

- Neither of its actions—*success* and *control*—are verbs; both are nominalizations.
- The subject is *success*, an abstraction.
- The sentence lacks flesh-and-blood characters.

We have to distinguish the literal meanings of *active* and *passive* from their figurative meanings before we can understand why we respond to those two sentences as we do.

We make sentences seem and be really passive when we combine passives with nominalizations:

Active-verbal:	*We* **INVESTIGATED** why *they* **INTERVIEWED** so few minority applicants.
Active-nominalized:	*We* CONDUCTED an **investigation** into why *they* DID so few **interviews** of minority applicants.
Passive-nominalized:	An **investigation** WAS CONDUCTED into why so few **interviews** WERE DONE.

Choosing Between Active and Passive

Some critics of style relentlessly urge us to avoid the passive because it adds a couple of words and often deletes the agent, the "doer" of the action, usually a main character. But in fact, the passive is often the better choice. To choose between active and passive, you have to answer three questions:

1. **Must your readers know who is responsible for the action?** Often, we won't say who does an action, because we don't know or readers won't care. For example, we naturally choose the passive in these sentences:

   ✓ The president **WAS RUMORED** to have considered resigning.

   ✓ Those who **ARE FOUND** guilty can **BE FINED.**

   ✓ Valuable records should always **BE KEPT** in a safe place.

   If we do not know who spread rumors, we cannot say, and no one doubts who finds people guilty or should keep records safe. So those passives are the right choice.

   Sometimes, of course, writers use the passive when they don't want readers to know who did an action, especially when the doer is the writer. For example,

   Because the test was not done, the flaw was uncorrected.

I will discuss the issue of deliberate impersonality in Lesson Ten.

2. **Would the active or passive verb help your readers move more smoothly from one sentence to the next?** We depend on the beginning of a sentence to give us a context of what we know before we follow the sentence to read what's new. A sentence confuses us when it starts with information that is new and unexpected. For example, in this next short passage, the subject of the second sentence gives us new and complex information (boldfaced) before we read more familiar information that we recall from the previous sentence (italicized):

> We must decide whether to improve education in the sciences alone or to raise the level of education across the whole curriculum. **The weight given to industrial competitiveness and the value we attach to the liberal arts**$_{\text{new information}}$ WILL INFLUENCE$_{\text{active verb}}$ *our decision*$_{\text{familiar information}}$.

In the second sentence, the verb *influence* is in the active voice. But we could follow the sentence more easily if it were passive, because the passive would put the short, familiar information first and the new and complex information last, the order we all prefer:

> ✓ We must decide whether to improve education in the sciences alone or raise the level of education across the whole curriculum. *Our decision*$_{\text{familiar information}}$ WILL BE INFLUENCED$_{\text{passive verb}}$ **by the weight we give to industrial competitiveness and the value we attach to the liberal arts**$_{\text{new information}}$.

I discuss the issue of old and new information in detail in the next lesson.

3. **Would the active or passive give your readers a more consistent and appropriate point of view?** The writer of this next passage reports the end of World War II in Europe from the point of view of the Allies. In so doing, she uses active verbs to make the Allies a consistent sequence of subjects:

✓ By early 1945, *the Allies* HAD essentially DEFEATED_{active} Germany; all that remained was a bloody climax. *American, French, British, and Russian forces* HAD BREACHED_{active} its borders and WERE BOMBING_{active} it around the clock. But *they* HAD not yet so DEVASTATED_{active} Germany as to destroy its ability to resist.

But if she had wanted us to understand history from the point of view of Germany, she would have used passive verbs to make Germany the subject/character:

✓ By early 1945, *Germany* HAD essentially BEEN DEFEATED_{passive}; all that remained was a bloody climax. *Its borders* HAD BEEN BREACHED_{passive}, and *it* WAS BEING BOMBED_{passive} around the clock. *It* HAD not BEEN SO DEVASTATED_{passive}, however, that *it* could not RESIST.

I'll discuss this issue again in the next lesson.

Here's the point: Many writers depend on the passive verb too much, but it has important uses. Use it when

- you don't know who did an action, your readers don't care, or you don't want them to know;
- you want to shift a long and complex bundle of information to the end of its sentence, especially when it also lets you move to its beginning a chunk of information that is shorter, more familiar, and therefore easier to understand;
- you want to focus your readers' attention on one or another character.

The "Objective" Passive

Some scholarly writers claim that by deleting a first-person subject, the passive voice creates an objective point of view, something like this:

Based on the writers' verbal intelligence, prior knowledge, and essay scores, their essays **WERE ANALYZED** for structure and evaluated for richness of concepts. The subjects **WERE** then **DIVIDED** into a high- or low-ability group. Half of each group **WAS** randomly **ASSIGNED** to a treatment group or to a placebo group.

Contrary to that claim, academic and scientific writers use the active voice and the first-person *I* and *we* regularly. These next passages come from articles in respected journals:

✓ This paper is concerned with two problems. How can **we** best handle in a transformational grammar certain restrictions that . . . , To illustrate, **we** may cite . . . , **we** shall show . . .

✓ Since the pituitary-adrenal axis is activated during the acute phase response, **we** have investigated the potential role . . . Specifically, **we** have studied the effects of interleukin-1 . . .

Here are the first few words from several consecutive sentences from *Science,* a journal of considerable prestige:

✓ **We** examine . . . **We** compare . . . **We** have used . . . Each has been weighted . . . **We** merely take . . . They are subject . . . **We** use . . . Efron and Morris describe . . . **We** observed . . . **We** might find . . .

> —John P. Gilbert, Bucknam McPeek, and Frederick Mosteller, "Statistics and Ethics in Surgery and Anesthesia," *Science*

Passives, Characters, and Metadiscourse

When academic writers do use the first person, however, they use it in certain ways. Look at the verbs in the passages above. There are two kinds:

- One kind refers to research activities: *study, investigate, examine, observe, use.* These verbs are usually in the passive voice: *The subjects WERE OBSERVED* . . .

- The other kind of verb refers not to the subject matter or the research, but to the writer's own writing and thinking:

cite, show, inquire. These verbs are often active and in the first person: *We* WILL SHOW . . .

You use what is called metadiscourse when you refer to

- your thinking and act of writing: *We/I will explain, show, argue, claim, deny, suggest, contrast, add, expand, summarize* . . .
- your certainty: *it seems, perhaps, undoubtedly, I think* . . .
- the logic and form of what you have written: *first, second; to begin; therefore, however, consequently* . . .
- your readers' actions: *consider now, as you recall, look at the next example* . . .

Metadiscourse appears most often in introductions, where writers announce their intentions: *I claim that* . . . , *I will show* . . . , *We begin by* . . . , and again at the end, when they summarize: *I have argued* . . . , *I have shown* . . .

On the other hand, scholarly writers use the first person less often to describe specific actions performed as *part* of the research. We rarely find passages like this:

To determine if monokines elicited an adrenal steroidogenic response, **I** ADDED preparations of . . .

The writer of the original sentence used a passive verb to name the action of adding because anyone can do that, not just the writer:

To determine if monokines elicited a response, **preparations** . . . WERE ADDED . . .

But a special problem lurks with a passive sentence: as did that writer, you can dangle a modifier. You dangle a modifier when you create an introductory phrase whose *implied* subject differs from the *explicit* subject in the following or preceding clause. In that example, the implied subject of the infinitive verb *determine* is *I* or *we: I determine* or *we determine.*

[So that **I** could] determine if monokines elicited a response, **preparations** . . . WERE ADDED . . .

But that implied subject differs from the *explicit* subject of the clause it introduces—*preparations*, as in *preparations were added*. When that happens, the modifier dangles. Writers of scientific prose use this pattern so often, however, that it has become standard usage in their community.

We might note that this impersonal "scientific" style is a modern development. In his "New Theory of Light and Colors" (1672), Sir Isaac Newton wrote this charming first-person account of an experiment:

> I procured a triangular glass prism, to try therewith the celebrated phenomena of colors. And for that purpose, having darkened my laboratory, and made a small hole in my window shade, to let in a convenient quantity of the sun's light, I placed my prism at the entrance, that the light might be thereby refracted to the opposite wall. It was at first a very pleasing diversion to view the vivid and intense colors produced thereby.

Here's the point: Some writers and editors resolutely avoid the first person by using the passive everywhere, but deleting an *I* or *we* doesn't make a scientist's thinking more objective. We know that behind those impersonal sentences are flesh-and-blood researchers doing, thinking, and writing. The first-person *I* and *we* are common in scholarly prose when used with verbs that name actions unique to the writer. Some critics frown on the expressions *I think . . . , I feel . . . , I believe . . .* because inexperienced writers use those words too often to introduce baseless opinion. But when used appropriately, the first person is entirely correct.

NOUN + NOUN + NOUN

One more stylistic choice does not directly involve characters and actions, but we discuss it here because it can distort the match that readers expect between the form of an idea and the grammar of its expression. It is the long compound noun phrase:

> Early *childhood thought disorder misdiagnosis* often results from unfamiliarity with recent *research literature* describing such conditions. This paper is a review of seven recent studies in which are findings of particular relevance to *pre-adolescent hyperactivity diagnosis* and to *treatment modalities* involving *medication maintenance level evaluation procedures*.

Some grammarians claim we should never modify one noun with another, but that would rule out common phrases such as *stone wall, student center, space shuttle,* and vast numbers of other useful terms.

But strings of nouns can feel lumpy, so avoid them. Especially avoid inventing your own. When you find a compound noun of your own invention, try revising, especially when the string includes nominalizations. To revise, just reverse the order of words and find prepositions to connect them:

1	2	3	4	5
early	childhood	thought	disorder	misdiagnosis
misdiagnose	disordered	thought	in early	childhood
5	4	3	1	2

Re-assembled, it looks like this:

Physicians misdiagnose[5] disordered[4] thought[3] in young[1] children[2] because they are unfamiliar with recent literature on the subject.

Here's the point: Whether you are a reader or a writer, you must understand three things about a style that seems complex:

- It may be necessary to express complex ideas precisely.
- It may needlessly complicate simple ideas.
- It may needlessly complicate already complex ideas.

Einstein said that everything should be made as simple as possible, but no simpler. But neither should it be made more complex. As a writer, your task is to recognize when you have committed that gratuitous complexity and, if you can, to revise it. When you do, you follow the Writer's Golden Rule: Write to others as you would have others write to you.

Cohesion and Coherence

*If he would inform, he must advance regularly from Things
known to things unknown, distinctly without Confusion,
and the lower he begins the better. It is a common Fault
in Writers, to allow their Readers too much knowledge:
They begin with that which should be the Middle, and skipping
backwards and forwards, 'tis impossible for any one but he
who is perfect in the Subject before, to understand their Work,
and such an one has no Occasion to read it.*
—BENJAMIN FRANKLIN

UNDERSTANDING COHERENCE

So far, I've discussed clarity as if we could achieve it just by
mapping characters and actions onto subjects and verbs. But
readers need more than individually clear sentences for a whole
passage to seem *coherent*. These two passages, for example, say
much the same thing but feel very different:

1a. The basis of our American democracy—equal opportunity for
all—is being threatened by college costs that have been rising
fast for the last several years. Increases in family income have
been significantly outpaced by increases in tuition at our col-
leges and universities during that period. Only the children of
the wealthiest families in our society will be able to afford a college education if this trend continues. Knowledge and intellectual skills, in addition to wealth, will divide us as a people, when

that happens. Equal opportunity and the egalitarian basis of our democratic society could be eroded by such a divide.

✓ 1b. In the last several years, college costs have been rising so fast that they are now threatening the basis of our American democracy—equal opportunity for all. During that period, tuition has significantly outpaced increases in family income. If this trend continues, a college education will soon be affordable only by the children of the wealthiest families in our society. When that happens, we will be divided as a people not only by wealth, but by knowledge and intellectual skills. Such a divide will erode equal opportunity and the egalitarian basis of our democratic society.

The first seems choppy, even disorganized; the second seems to "hang together" better.

But like the word *clarity*, the words *choppy* and *disorganized* refer not to what is on the page, but to how what is on the page makes us *feel*. What is it about the *arrangement* of words in (1a) that makes us feel that we are moving through it in fits and starts? Why does (1b) seem to flow so much more easily? We base those judgments on two aspects of word order:

- We judge sequences of sentences to be *cohesive* depending on how each sentence ends and the next begins.
- We judge a whole passage to be *coherent* depending on how all the sentences in a passage cumulatively begin.

Cohesion: A Sense of Flow

In Lesson Four, we devoted a few pages (pp. 44–47) to that familiar advice, "Avoid passives." If we always did, we would choose the active verb in sentence (2a) below over the passive in (2b):

2a. The collapse of a dead star into a point perhaps no larger than a marble **CREATES**_{active} a black hole.

2b. A black hole **IS CREATED**_{passive} by the collapse of a dead star into a point perhaps no larger than a marble.

But we might choose otherwise if we had to put one of those sentences between these two:

[1]Some astonishing questions about the nature of the universe have been raised by scientists studying black holes in space. [2a/b][———]. [3]So much matter compressed into so little volume changes the fabric of space around it in puzzling ways.

Here's the active sentence there:

> 1a. [1]Some astonishing questions about the nature of the universe have been raised by scientists studying black holes in space. [2a]The collapse of a dead star into a point perhaps no larger than a marble creates a black hole. [3]So much matter compressed into so little volume changes the fabric of space around it in puzzling ways.

And here's the passive:

> 1b. [1]Some astonishing questions about the nature of the universe have been raised by scientists studying <u>black holes</u> in space. [2b]A <u>black hole</u> is created by the collapse of <u>a dead star</u> into a point perhaps <u>no larger than a marble</u>. [3]<u>So much matter compressed into so little volume</u> changes the fabric of space around it in puzzling ways.

Our sense of "flow" should call not for (2a), the sentence with the active verb, but for (2b), the one with the passive.

The reason is clear: the last four words of the first sentence introduce an important new character—*black holes in space:*

> [1]Some astonishing questions about the nature of the universe have been raised by scientists studying **black holes in space.**

If we follow it with sentence (2a), the first concepts we hit are collapsed stars and marbles, information that seems to come out of nowhere:

> [1] . . . universe have been raised by scientists studying black holes in space. [2a]**The collapse of a dead star into a point perhaps no larger than a marble** creates . . .

But if we follow sentence (1) with (2b), the sentence with the passive verb, we connect them more smoothly, because now the first words we hit in (2b) pick up on what we just read at the end of (1):

[1] . . . studying **black holes in space. [2b]A black hole** is created by the collapse of . . .

Note too that the passive also lets us put at the *end* of sentence (2b) words that connect it to the *beginning* of sentence (3):

[1] . . . black holes in space. [2b]A black hole is created by the collapse of a dead star into **a point perhaps no larger than a marble. [3]So much matter compressed into so little volume** changes the fabric of space around it in puzzling ways.

The passive sentence, (2b), is the better choice.

Here's the point: We feel a sentence is cohesive with the one before it when we see at the beginning of the second sentence information that appeared toward the end of the first. That's what gives us our experience of "flow." And in fact, that's the biggest reason the passive is in the language: to arrange sentences so that they flow from one to the next easily.

DIAGNOSIS AND REVISION

That principle of reading suggests two principles of revision. They are mirror images of each other. The first is this:

1. **Begin sentences with information familiar to your readers.** Readers get that familiar information from two sources: first, they remember words from the sentence they just read. That's why the beginning of sentence (2b) about black holes coheres with the end of (1) and why the beginning of (3) coheres with the end of (2b):

   [1] . . . questions about the nature of the universe have been raised by scientists studying **[black holes in space. [2b]A black hole]** is created by the collapse of a dead star into **[a point per-**

haps no larger than a marble. ³So much matter compressed into so little volume] changes the fabric of space . . .

Second, readers bring to a sentence a general knowledge of its subject. We would not have been surprised, for example, if a sentence (4) in that series about black holes had begun like this:

. . . changes the fabric of space around it in puzzling ways. **⁴Astronomers have reported** that . . .

The word *Astronomers* did not appear in the preceding sentence, but since we are reading about space, we wouldn't be surprised by a reference to them.

The second principle is the flip side of the first.

2. **End sentences with information readers cannot anticipate.** Readers always prefer to read what's easy before what's hard, and what is familiar and simple is easier to understand than what is new and complex.

You can more easily see when others fail to observe those principles in their writing than you can in your own, because after you've worked on your own for a while, it all seems familiar—to you. But hard as it is to distinguish old from new in your own writing, you have to try, because readers want to begin sentences with information that is familiar to *them*, and only then move on to information that is new.

Here's the point: In every *sequence* of sentences you write, you have to balance principles that make individual sentences in a passage clear and principles that make the whole passage cohesive. *But in that tradeoff, give priority to helping readers create a sense of cohesive flow.* That means starting sentences with information that readers are familiar with. Fortunately, this principle about old and new information cooperates with the principle of characters as subjects. Once you mention your main characters, readers take them as familiar information. So when you regularly get characters up front, you also get up front familiar information.

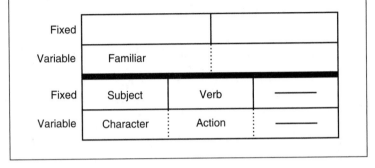

Coherence: A Sense of the Whole

When you create cohesive flow, you take the first step toward helping readers think your prose hangs together. But they will judge you to be a good writer only when they feel that your writing is not just cohesive but *coherent*, a quality different from cohesion. It's easy to confuse the words *cohesion* and *coherence* because they sound so much alike.

- Think of *cohesion* as pairs of sentences fitting together the way two Lego® pieces do (recall the black hole sentences).
- Think of *coherence* as seeing what all the sentences in a piece of writing add up to, the way a hundred Lego® pieces create a building, bridge, or boat.

This next passage has great cohesive "flow" because we move from the end of each sentence to the next without a hitch:

Sayner, Wisconsin, is the snowmobile capital of the world. The buzzing of snowmobile engines fills the air, and their tanklike tracks crisscross the snow. The snow reminds me of Mom's mashed potatoes, covered with furrows I would draw with my fork. Her mashed potatoes usually make me sick—that's why I play with them. I like to make a hole in the middle of the potatoes and fill it with melted butter. This behavior has been the subject of long chats between me and my analyst.

Though we can get from each of those sentences to the next easily, that passage as a whole is incoherent. (It was created by six different writers, one of whom wrote the first sentence, with the other five sequentially adding one sentence knowing only the immediately preceding one.) It is incoherent for three reasons:

1. Subjects of the sentences do not make up a set of related topics.
2. The sentences share no common "themes" or ideas.
3. Taken together, the sentences fail to focus on a single point. The paragraph has no one sentence that states what the whole passage supports or explains.

I will discuss that second point in the next lesson. The rest of this lesson focuses on the first point, shared subjects.

Subjects, Topics, Grammar, and Coherence

For five hundred years, English teachers have defined *subject* in two ways:

1. the "doer" of the action
2. what a sentence is "about," its main topic

In Lessons Three and Four, we saw why that first definition doesn't work: the subjects of many sentences are actions.

But also flawed is that second schoolbook definition: "A subject is what a sentence is about." It is flawed because often, the subject of a sentence doesn't state its main topic, the idea that the rest of the sentence "comments" on; that function can be performed by other parts of a sentence. For example:

- The subject of this sentence (italicized) is *it*, but its topic (boldfaced) is *your claim*, the object of the preposition *for:*

    It is impossible for **your claim** to be proved.

- The subject of this sentence is *I*, but its topic is *this question*, the object of *to*:

    In regard to **this question,** *I* believe more research is needed.

- The subject of this sentence is *it*, but its topic is *our proposal*, the subject of a verb in a subordinate clause:

    It is likely that **our proposal** will be accepted.

- The subject of this sentence is *no one*, but its topic is *such results*, a direct object shifted to the front for emphasis:

    Such results *no one* could have predicted.

Here's the point: We use the term *topic* to mean what a sentence is "about," but that topic is not always its grammatical subject. *But readers expect it to be.* They judge writing to be clear and direct when they quickly see topics and subject/characters in the same words.

Diagnosing and Revising Topics

This passage feels choppy, out of focus, even disorganized:

> The particular ideas toward the beginning of sentences define what a passage is "about" for a reader. Moving through a paragraph from a coherent point of view is made possible by a sequence of topics that constitute a limited set of related ideas. A seeming absence of context for each sentence is one consequence of making random shifts in topics. Feelings of dislocation, disorientation, and lack of focus in a passage occur when that happens.

Here's how to diagnose its problems and revise it.

1. **Diagnose:**
    a. Underline the first seven or eight words of every sentence in the passage.

b. If you can, underline the first five or six words of every clause in those sentences, both subordinate and main.

> <u>The particular ideas toward the beginning of sentences</u> define what a passage is "about" for a reader. <u>Moving through a paragraph from a coherent point of view</u> is made possible by a sequence of topics that constitute a limited set of related ideas. <u>A seeming absence of context for each sentence</u> is one consequence of making random shifts in topics. <u>Feelings of dislocation, disorientation, and lack of focus in a passage</u> occur when that happens.

2. **Analyze:**

   a. Do the underlined words constitute a relatively small set of related ideas? Even if *you* see how they are related, will your readers? For that passage, the answer is no.

   b. Do those words name the most important characters, real or abstract? Again, the answer is no.

   c. What are the main topic/characters? Try giving the passage a title. Some of its words will identify what should be the topics of most of the sentences. In this case, the title would be something like "Readers' Responses to Consistent and Inconsistent Topics."

3. **Revise:**

   a. In most (not necessarily all) of the sentences, use subjects to name those topics.

   b. Put those subjects close to the beginning of the sentences.

Here is that passage revised.

> **Readers** look for consistent topics of sentences to tell them what a whole passage is "about." If **they** feel that its sequence of topics focuses on a limited set of related topics, then **they** will feel they are moving through that passage from a coherent point of view. But if **topics** seem to shift randomly, then **readers** have to begin each sentence from no coherent point of view, and when that happens, **they** feel dislocated and disoriented, and the **passage** seems out of focus.

The Difficult Craft of Beginning a Sentence Well

It's hard to begin a sentence well. Readers want to get to topic/subjects quickly, but too often, writers begin sentences in ways that keep readers from getting there. It's called *throat-clearing.* Throat-clearing typically begins with metadiscourse that connects a sentence to the previous one, with transitions such as *and, but, therefore:*

> And therefore . . .

We then add a second kind of metadiscourse that expresses our attitude toward what is coming, words such as *fortunately, perhaps, allegedly, it is important to note, for the most part,* or *politically speaking:*

> And therefore, politically speaking . . .

Then we can indicate time, place, or manner:

> And therefore, politically speaking, in Eastern states since 1980 . . .

Only then do we get to the topic/subject:

> And, therefore, politically speaking, in Eastern states since 1980, **acid rain** has become a serious problem.

When you open several sentences like that, your readers have a hard time seeing not just what your individual sentences are "about," but the cumulative focus of a whole passage. When you find a sentence with lots of words before its subject/topic, revise:

> ✓ Since 1980, therefore, **acid rain** has become a serious political problem in Eastern states.

Here's the point: In most of your sentences (not necessarily all), start with the subject and make that subject the topic of the sentence.

Integrating the Principles

We can bring together these principles about old and new and consistent topic strings with the principles about characters as subjects and actions as verbs (I'll fill in the empty boxes in Lesson Six):

Fixed	Topic		
Variable	Familiar		
Fixed	Subject	Verb	———
Variable	Character	Action	———

No unit of information is shorter and simpler than the name of a familiar character. So when you create a sequence of subjects out of a limited set of characters, real or abstract, you create a sequence of topics that your readers will think is clear and consistent, and that helps them create a sense of coherence.

6

Emphasis

In the end is my beginning.
—T. S. ELIOT

UNDERSTANDING EMPHASIS

If you consistently write sentences whose subject/topics name a few central characters and then join them to strong verbs, you'll likely get the rest of the sentence right, and in the process create a passage that seems both cohesive and coherent. But if the first few words of a sentence are worth special attention, so are the last few, because how you end a sentence determines how readers judge both its clarity and its strength. In this lesson, we address clarity first, then strength, then how the right emphasis on the right words can contribute to a kind of coherence even more global than the coherence we get from consistent topics.

When readers get up speed in a sentence's first words, they more easily get through complicated material that follows. Compare:

1a. A sociometric and actuarial analysis of Social Security revenues and disbursements for the last six decades to determine changes in projecting deficits is the subject of this study.

✓ 1b. In this study, we analyze Social Security's revenues and disbursements for the last six decades, using sociometric and actuarial criteria to determine changes in projecting deficits.

As we start (1a), we struggle to understand its technical terms at the same time we are hacking through a twenty-two-word subject before we get to a verb. In (1b), we go through just five words to get past a subject and verb and twelve more before we hit a term that might slow us up. By that point we have enough momentum to carry us through the complexity to its end. In short, in (1a), we hit the complexity at the beginning; in (1b), we don't hit it until near the end, where we handle it better.

There are, however, two kinds of complexity: grammar and meaning.

Complex Grammar

Which of these two sentences do you prefer?

> 2a. Lincoln's claim that the Civil War was God's punishment of both North and South for slavery appears in the last part of the speech.

> ✓ 2b. In the last part of his speech, Lincoln claims that God gave the Civil War to both North and South as a punishment for slavery.

Most readers dislike (2a) because it begins with a long, complex grammatical subject. We prefer (2b) because it begins simply, then moves toward complexity.

Complex Terms

Readers have a problem with all kinds of unfamiliar technical terms, but especially when those new terms appear toward the beginning of a sentence. Compare these two passages:

> 3a. The role of calcium blocker drugs in the control of cardiac irregularity can be seen through an understanding of the role of calcium in the activation of muscle cells. The regulatory proteins actin, myosin, tropomyosin, and troponin make up the sarcomere, the basic unit of muscle contraction. ATPase, the energy-producing protein myosin, makes up its thick filament, while actin, tropomyosin, and troponin make up its thin filament. Interaction of myosin and actin triggers muscle contraction.

✓ 3b. When a muscle contracts, it uses calcium. We must therefore understand how calcium affects muscle cells to understand how cardiac irregularity is controlled by drugs called "calcium blockers." The basic unit of muscle contraction is the sarcomere. It has two filaments, one thin and one thick. Those filaments consist of four proteins that regulate contraction: actin, myosin, tropomyosin, and troponin. Muscles contract when the protein in the thin filament, actin, interacts with the protein myosin in the thick filament, an energy-producing or ATPase protein.

Both passages use the same technical terms, but (3b) is clearer to those who know nothing about the chemistry of muscles.

Those passages differ in two ways. First, information that is implicit in (3a) I stated explicitly in (3b):

3a. . . . and troponin make up the sarcomere, the basic unit of muscle contraction. ATPase, the energy-producing protein myosin, makes up . . .

✓ 3b. The basic unit of muscle contraction is the sarcomere. It has two filaments, one thin and one thick. . . .

More important, I moved the technical terms from the beginning of the sentences in (3a) to the end of the sentences in (3b). Note how almost all the technical terms in (3a) are at the beginning of their sentences:

3a. The role of **calcium blocker drugs** in the control of **cardiac irregularity** can be seen through an understanding of the role of calcium in the activation of muscle cells.

The regulatory proteins actin, myosin, tropomyosin, and troponin make up the **sarcomere,** the basic unit of muscle contraction.

ATPase, the energy-producing protein myosin, makes up its thick filament, while **actin, tropomyosin, and troponin** make up its thin filament.

Interaction of myosin and actin triggers muscle contraction.

In (3b), those technical terms appear at the ends of their sentences:

. . . uses **calcium.**

. . . controlled by drugs called **"calcium blockers."**

. . . is the **sarcomere.**

. . . four proteins that regulate contraction: **actin, myosin, tropomyosin, and troponin.**

. . . in the thick filament, an **energy-producing or ATPase protein.**

These principles work for prose intended even for professional readers. In this next passage, from the *New England Journal of Medicine,* the writer deliberately uses metadiscourse to construct the second sentence just to get a new technical term at its end:

> The incubation of peripheral-blood lymphocytes with a lymphokine, interleukin-2, generates lymphoid cells that can lyse fresh, noncultured, natural-killer-cell-resistant tumor cells but not normal cells. *We term these cells* **lymphokine-activated killer (LAK) cells.**

Here's the point: Your readers want you to use the end of your sentences to help them manage two kinds of difficulty:

- long and complex phrases and clauses, and
- new information, particularly unfamiliar technical terms.

We can add those two points to our schematic layout of a clear and direct sentence.

Fixed	Topic		
Variable	Short, simple, familiar		New, long, complex
Fixed	Subject	Verb	———
Variable	Character	Action	———

One More New Term: Stress

In the last lesson, we said that an important position in the *psychological* geography of a sentence is its first few words, because they name the topic of a sentence, its psychological subject (see pp. 59–60.) I've been discussing the end of a sentence in general, but the last few words are particularly important. You can sense that importance when you hear your voice rise and emphasize one syllable more strongly than you do the others:

. . . more strongly than you do the ^{6}-thers.

We have the same experience even when reading silently.

We'll call this most emphatic part of a sentence its stress and add it to our last box. How you manage the emphasis in that stress position helps establish the voice readers hear in your prose.

Fixed	Topic		Stress
Variable	Short, simple, familiar		New, long, complex
Fixed	Subject	Verb	———
Variable	Character	Action	———

In Lesson Four, we saw how it was possible to manipulate subject/topics to create different points of view (pp. 46–47). To create different effects, you can manipulate the stress of a sentence as well.

Compare these passages. One was written to blame an American president for being weak with Iran on arms control. The other is my revision; it seems to blame Iran. You can tell which is which if you thump your finger as you read the boldface words at the ends of the sentences:

1a. The administration has blurred an issue central to arms control, **the issue of verification.** Irresponsible charges, innuendo, and leaks have submerged **serious problems with Iranian com-**

pliance. The objective, instead, should be not to exploit these concerns in order to further poison our relations, repudiate existing agreements, or, worse still, terminate arms control altogether, but to **insist on compliance and clarify questionable behavior.**

1b. The issue of verification—so central to arms control—has been **blurred by the administration.** Serious problems with Iranian compliance have been submerged in **irresponsible charges, innuendo, and leaks.** The objective, instead, should be to clarify questionable behavior and insist on compliance—not to exploit these concerns in order to **further poison our relations, repudiate existing agreements, or, worse still, terminate arms control altogether.**

Here's the point: Just as you look at the first few words of your sentences for point of view, you can look at the last few words for special emphasis. You can manipulate a sentence to emphasize particular words that you want readers to hear stressed and thereby note as particularly significant.

DIAGNOSIS AND REVISION

If you have managed your subjects and topics well, you will almost by default emphasize the right words at the end of your sentences. But there are some ways to revise just for that purpose.

Three Tactical Revisions

1. **Trim the end.**

Sociobiologists claim that our genes control our social behavior **in the way we act in situations we are in every day.**

Since *social behavior* means *the way we act in situations . . . ,* we drop everything after *behavior:*

✓ Sociobiologists claim that our genes **control our social behavior.**

2. **Shift peripheral ideas to the left.**

> The data offered to prove ESP are too weak **for the most part.**
>
> ✓ **For the most part,** the data offered to prove ESP are **too weak.**

Particularly avoid ending with anticlimactic metadiscourse:

> Job opportunities in computer programming are getting scarcer, **it must be remembered.**
>
> ✓ **It must be remembered** that job opportunities in computer programming are getting scarcer.

3. **Shift new information to the right.** A more common way to manage stress is by moving new information to the end of a sentence.

> **Questions about the ethics of withdrawing intravenous feeding** are *more difficult* [than something just mentioned].
>
> ✓ *More difficult* [than something just mentioned] are **questions about the ethics of withdrawing intravenous feeding.**

Six Syntactic Devices to Enhance Emphasis

1. **Passives (for the last time)**   A passive verb lets you flip a subject and object. Compare these next two sentences. To stress the concept of genes influencing behavior, we revise the active verb into a passive to get that idea closer to the stress position:

> Some sociobiologists claim that **our genes** influence$_{active}$ aspects of behavior that we think are learned. **Our genes,** for example, seem to determine . . .
>
> ✓ Some sociobiologists claim that aspects of behavior that we think are learned are in fact influenced$_{passive}$ **by our genes. Our genes,** for example, seem to determine . . .

As we've seen, the passive is in the language so that we can get old and new information in the right order.

2. ***There***   Some editors discourage *there is/there are* constructions, but if you never used one, you'd lose a device that lets
you shift a phrase toward the end of its sentence. Compare:

> Several syntactic devices let you manage where in a sentence
> you locate units of new information.

> ✓ **There are** several syntactic devices that let you manage where
> in a sentence you locate units of new information.

Experienced writers regularly use *there* at the beginning of
a paragraph to introduce concepts that they develop in sentences that follow.

3. ***What*-shift**   This is another device that shifts a part of the
sentence to the right:

> We need a monetary policy that would end fluctuations in
> money supply, unemployment, and inflation.

> ✓ **What** we need **is** a monetary policy that would end fluctuations
> in money supply, unemployment, and inflation.

4. ***It*-shift**   When you have a subject consisting of a long noun
clause, you can move it to the end of the sentence and start
with an *it:*

> **That oil prices would be set by OPEC** once seemed inevitable.

> ✓ *It* once seemed inevitable **that oil prices would be set by
> OPEC.**

5. ***Not only X, but Y (as well)***   In this next pair, note how the
but emphasizes the last element of the pair:

> We must clarify these issues and **develop trust.**

> ✓ We must *not only* clarify these issues, *but* **develop trust.**

Unless you have reason to emphasize the negative, end with
the positive:

> The point is to highlight our success, **not to emphasize our
> failures.**

> ✓ The point is not to emphasize our failures but **to highlight our
> success.**

The cost of these five devices is a few extra words, so use them sparingly.

6. **Repeated words and pronoun substitution**   This is a fine point: a sentence can end flatly if you repeat a word that you used just a few words before at the end of a sentence, because the voice we hear in our mind's ear drops off at the end of a sentence. If you read aloud the preceding sentence, this one, and the next, you can hear that drop at the end the sentence. To avoid that kind of flatness, rewrite or use a pronoun instead of repeating the word at the end of the sentence. For example:

> A sentence will seem to end flatly if you use a word at its end that you used just a few words before, because when you repeat that word, your voice **drops.** Instead of repeating the noun, use a **pronoun.** The reader will at least hear emphasis on the word just **before** *it.*

Topics, Emphasis, Themes, and Coherence

There is one more function performed by the stress of certain sentences, one that is important in helping readers think a passage is coherent. As we saw in the last lesson, readers take the clearest topic to be a short noun phrase that comes early in a sentence, usually as its subject. That's why most of us judge this next paragraph to be unfocused: its sentences do not open from any consistent point of view. After you read this passage, skim its topics:

1a. Great strides in the early and accurate diagnosis of Alzheimer's disease have been made in recent years. Not too long ago, senility in an older patient who seemed to be losing touch with reality was often confused with Alzheimer's. Genetic clues have become the basis of newer and more reliable tests in the last few years, however. The risk of human tragedy of another kind, though, has resulted from the increasing accuracy of these tests: predictions about susceptibility to Alzheimer's have become possible, long before the appearance of any overt symptoms. At that point, an apparently healthy person could be devastated by such an early diagnosis.

If we revise that passage to make the topics more consistent, we make it more coherent:

> ✓ 1b. In recent years, **researchers** have made great strides in the early and accurate diagnosis of Alzheimer's disease. Not too long ago, when **a physician** examined an older patient who seemed out of touch with reality, **she** had to guess whether the **person** was senile or had Alzheimer's. In the past few years, however, **physicians** have been able to use new and more reliable tests focusing on genetic clues. But in **the accuracy of these new tests** lies the risk of another kind of human tragedy: **physicians** may be able to predict Alzheimer's long before its overt appearance, but **such an early diagnosis** could psychologically devastate an apparently healthy person.

The topics in that passage now focus on just two topics: researcher/physicians and testing/diagnosis.

But there is one more revision that would make that passage even more of a whole. This passage is not centrally about advances in diagnosis, as stated in the first sentence, but about their potential risks. That concept, however, does not appear in that paragraph until we are more than halfway through it.

Readers would understand that passage better if its key concepts appeared in the first sentence, and (here is where it gets tricky) *specifically toward the end of that opening sentence.* Readers read the opening sentence or two of a paragraph to find the key concepts that the paragraph will repeat and develop, *and they look for those concepts in the last few words* of their opening sentences.

A new first sentence for the Alzheimer's paragraph would help readers pull the whole passage together around the key concepts not just of *Alzheimer's* and *new diagnoses,* but the concepts *new problem* and *informing those most at risk.*

> In recent years, though researchers have made great strides in the early and accurate diagnosis of Alzheimer's disease, those **diagnoses** have raised **a new problem** about **informing those most at risk before they show symptoms of it.**

We can call those key words that run through a passage its *themes.*

Look at the highlighted words in the passage below one more time:

- The boldfaced words are all about testing.
- The italicized words are all about mental states.
- The capitalized words are all about a new problem.

Each of those concepts is announced toward the end of a new opening sentence, especially the theme of the new problem.

> ✓ 1b. In recent years, though researchers have made great strides in the early and accurate **diagnosis** of *Alzheimer's disease,* those **diagnoses** have raised A NEW PROBLEM about INFORMING THOSE *MOST AT RISK* BEFORE THEY SHOW *SYMPTOMS OF IT*. Not too long ago, when a physician examined an older patient who seemed *out of touch with reality,* she had to **guess** whether that person had *Alzheimer's* or was *only senile*. In the past few years, however, physicians have been able to use **new and more reliable tests** focusing on genetic clues. But in the accuracy of these **new tests** lies the RISK OF ANOTHER KIND OF HUMAN TRAGEDY: physicians may be able to **predict** *Alzheimer's* long before its overt appearance, but such an early **diagnosis** could PSYCHOLOGICALLY DEVASTATE AN APPARENTLY HEALTHY PERSON.

That passage now "hangs together" not for just one reason, but for three:

- Its topics consistently focus on physicians and diagnosis.
- Running through it are strings of words that focus on the themes of (1) tests, (2) mental conditions, and (3) a new problem.
- *And no less important, the opening sentence prepares us to notice those themes by emphasizing them at the end of its opening sentence.*

This principle applies not just to sentences that introduce individual paragraphs, but to sentences that introduce passages of any length: *locate at the end of an introductory sentence words that announce the key concepts that you intend to develop in the rest of the passage.*

Here's the point: We depend on concepts running through a passage to create a sense of coherence. You help readers identify those concepts in two ways:

- Repeat them as topics of sentences, usually as subjects.
- Repeat them as themes elsewhere in a passage in nouns, verbs, and adjectives.

Readers are more likely to notice those themes if you state them at the end of the sentence that introduces a passage, in its stress position.

Concision

To a Snail:
If "compression is the first grace of style," you have it.
—MARIANNE MOORE

UNDERSTANDING CONCISION

You are close to clarity when you match characters and actions to subjects and verbs, and closer yet when you get the right characters into topics and the right words under stress. But readers may still think your prose is a long way from graceful if it's anything like this:

> In my personal opinion, it is necessary that we should not ignore the opportunity to think over each and every suggestion offered.

That writer matched characters with subjects, and actions with verbs, but in too many words: opinion is always personal, so we don't need *personal*, and since this whole statement is opinion, we don't even need *in my opinion*. *Think over* means *consider*. *Each and every* is redundant. A suggestion is by definition offered, and *not ignore* means *consider*. In fewer words,

✓ We should consider each suggestion.

Though not elegant, that sentence at least has style's first grace—that of compression, or as we'll call it, *concision*. Concision, though, is only a start. You must still make your sentences shapely. In this lesson, I focus on concision; in the next, on shape.

DIAGNOSIS AND REVISION

Five Principles of Concision

When I edited that sentence about suggestions, I applied five principles:

1. Delete words that mean little or nothing.
2. Delete words that repeat the meaning of other words.
3. Delete words implied by other words.
4. Replace a phrase with a word.
5. Change negatives to affirmatives.

Those principles are easy to state but hard to follow, because you have to inch your way through every word in every sentence you write, cutting here, compressing there, and that's labor-intensive. Those five principles, though, can guide you in that work.

1. Delete Meaningless Words   Some words are verbal tics that we use as unconsciously as we clear our throats:

kind of   actually   particular   really   certain   various
virtually   individual   basically   generally   given   practically

Productivity **actually** depends on **certain** factors that **basically** involve psychology more than **any particular** technology.

✓ Productivity depends on psychology more than on technology.

2. Delete Doubled Words   Early in the history of English, writers often paired a French or Latin word with a native English one, because foreign words sounded more learned. Now they are just redundant. Among the common pairs:

full and complete	hope and trust	any and all
true and accurate	each and every	basic and fundamental
hopes and desires	first and foremost	various and sundry

3. Delete What Readers Can Infer   This is a common redundancy but hard to identify, because it comes in so many forms.

Redundant Modifiers   Often, the meaning of a word implies its modifier:

> Do not try to *predict* those **future** events that will **completely** *revolutionize* society, because **past** *history* shows that it is the **final** *outcome* of minor events that **unexpectedly** *surprises* us more.

✓ Do not try to predict revolutionary events, because history shows that the outcome of minor events surprises us more.

Some common redundancies:

terrible tragedy	various different	free gift
basic fundamentals	future plans	each individual
final outcome	true facts	consensus of opinion

Redundant Categories   Every word implies its general category, so you can usually cut a word that names it. Compare (the category is boldfaced):

> During that *period* **of time,** the *membrane* **area** became *pink* **in color** and *shiny* **in appearance.**

✓ During that *period,* the *membrane* became *pink* and *shiny.*

When you do that, you may have to change an adjective into an adverb:

> The holes must be aligned in an *accurate* **manner.**

✓ The holes must be aligned *accurately.*

Sometimes you change an adjective into a noun:

> The county manages the *educational* **system** and *public recreational* **activities.**

✓ The county manages *education* and *public recreation.*

Here are some general nouns (boldfaced) often used redundantly:

large in **size**	round in **shape**	honest in **character**
unusual in **nature**	of a strange **type**	**area** of mathematics
of a bright **color**	at an early **time**	in a confused **state**

General Implications   This kind of wordiness is even harder to spot because it can be so diffuse:

Imagine someone trying to learn the rules for playing chess.

Learn implies *trying, playing a game* implies *rules.* More concisely,

Imagine learning the rules of chess.

4. Replace a Phrase with a Word   This redundancy is especially difficult to fix, because you need a big vocabulary and the wit to use it. For example:

As you carefully read what you have written to improve wording and catch errors of spelling and punctuation, the thing to do before anything else is to see whether you could use sequences of subjects and verbs instead of the same ideas expressed in nouns.

That is,

✓ As you edit, first replace nominalizations with clauses.

I compressed five phrases into five words:

carefully read what you have written	→	edit
the thing to do before anything else	→	first
use X instead of Y	→	replace
nouns instead of verbs	→	nominalizations
sequences of subjects and verbs	→	clauses

I can offer no principle to tell you when to replace a phrase with a word, much less give you the word. I can point out only that you often can, and that you should be alert for opportunities to do so—which is to say, try.

Here are some common phrases (boldfaced) to watch for. Note that some of these let you turn a nominalization into a verb (both italicized):

We must explain **the reason for** the *delay* in the meeting.

✓ We must explain **why** the meeting is *delayed*.

Despite the fact that the data were checked, errors occurred.

✓ **Even though** the data were checked, errors occurred.

In the event that you finish early, contact this office.

✓ **If** you finish early, contact this office.

In a situation where a class is closed, you may petition for admission.

✓ **When** a class is closed, you may petition for admission.

I want to say a few words **concerning the matter of** money.

✓ I want to say a few words **about** money.

There is a need for more careful *inspection* of all welds.

✓ You **must** *inspect* all welds more carefully.

We **are in a position** to make you an offer.

✓ We **can** make you an offer.

It is possible that nothing will come of this.

✓ Nothing **may** come of this.

Prior to the *end* of the training, apply for your license.

✓ **Before** training *ends,* apply for your license.

We have noted a **decrease/increase in** the number of errors.

✓ We have noted *fewer/more* errors.

5. Change Negatives to Affirmatives   When you express an idea in a negative form, not only must you use an extra word: *same → not different,* but you also force readers to do a kind of algebraic factoring. These two sentences, for example, mean much the same thing, but the affirmative is more direct:

> Do not write in the negative. → Write in the affirmative.

Do not translate a negative into an affirmative if you want to emphasize the negative. (Is that such a sentence? I could have written, *Keep a negative sentence when . . .*) But you can rewrite most negatives, some formulaically:

not different	→	similar	not many	→	few
not the same	→	different	not often	→	rarely
not allow	→	prevent	not stop	→	continue
not notice	→	overlook	not include	→	omit

Some verbs, prepositions, and conjunctions are implicitly negative:

Verbs	*preclude, prevent, lack, fail, doubt, reject, avoid, deny, refuse, exclude, contradict, prohibit, bar*
Prepositions	*without, against, lacking, but for, except*
Conjunctions	*unless, except when*

You can baffle readers if you combine *not* with these negative words. Compare these:

> **Except** when applicants have **failed** to submit applications **without** documentation, benefits will **not** be **denied.**

✓ You will receive benefits only if you submit your documents.

✓ To receive benefits, submit your documents.

And you baffle readers completely when you combine explicitly and implicitly negative words with passives and nominalizations:

> There should be **no** submission of payments **without** notification of this office, **unless** the payment does **not** exceed $100.

> Do not **submit** payments if you have not **notified** this office, unless you are **paying** less than $100.

Now revise the negatives into affirmatives:

✓ If you pay more than $100, notify this office first.

Here's the point: Readers think you write clearly when you use only the words you need to say what you mean.

1. Delete words that mean little or nothing.
2. Delete words that repeat the meaning of other words.
3. Delete words implied by other words.
4. Replace a phrase with a word.
5. Change negatives to affirmatives.

A Particular Kind of Redundancy: Metadiscourse

In Lesson Four, I described metadiscourse as language we use to refer to

- the writer's intentions: *to sum up, candidly, I believe*
- the writer's confidence: *may, perhaps, certainly, must*
- directions to the reader: *note that, consider now, as you see*
- the structure of the text: *first, second, finally, therefore, however*

Everything you write needs metadiscourse, but too much buries your ideas:

> The last point I would like to make is that in regard to men-women relationships, it is important to keep in mind that the greatest changes have occurred in how they work together.

Only nine words in that sentence address men-women relationships:

> men-women relationships . . . greatest changes . . . how they work together.

The rest is metadiscourse:

> The last point I would like to make is that in regard to . . . it is important to keep in mind that . . .

When we prune metadiscourse, we tighten the sentence:

> The greatest changes in men-women relationships have occurred in how they work together.

Now that we see what the sentence says, we can make it still more direct:

> ✓ Finally, men and women have changed their relationships most in how they work together.

Some teachers and editors urge us to cut all metadiscourse, but everything we write needs some. You have to read with an eye to how good writers in your field use it, then do likewise. There are, however, some types that you can usually cut.

Metadiscourse That Attributes Your Ideas to a Source   Don't announce that something has been anonymously *observed, noticed, noted,* and so on; just state the fact:

> High divorce rates **have been observed** to occur in areas that **have been determined to have** low population density.
> ✓ High divorce rates occur in areas with low population density.

Metadiscourse That Announces Your Topic   The boldface phrases tell your reader what your sentence is "about":

> **This section introduces another** problem, that of noise pollution. **The first thing to say about it is** that noise pollution exists not only . . .

You help readers catch a topic more easily if you reduce the metadiscourse:

> ✓ **Another** problem is noise pollution. **First**, it exists not only . . .

You can use two other constructions to call attention to a word or phrase, usually mentioned at least once before:

> **In regard to** a vigorous style, the most important feature is a short, concrete subject followed by a forceful verb.

> **So far as** China's industrial development **is concerned,** it will take only a few years to equal that of Japan.

But you can usually get those topics into a subject:

- ✓ The most important feature of a vigorous style is a short, concrete subject followed by a forceful verb.
- ✓ China will take only a few years to equal Japan's industrial development.

Look hard at a sentence opening with a metadiscourse subject and verb that merely announce a topic:

> In this essay, **I will discuss** the role of metaphor in style.

I write that kind of sentence when I have no idea where I am going, saying in effect, "I have this topic and hope I eventually think of something to say about it." On the other hand, that kind of sentence in a professional journal promises to develop what it names.

Excessive Hedging and Intensifying   This kind of metadiscourse can not only be redundant, but influence how readers judge your character, because it signals how well you balance caution and confidence.

Hedges   These are common hedges:

Adverbs	*usually, often, sometimes, almost, virtually, possibly, perhaps, apparently, in some ways, to a certain extent, somewhat, in some/certain respects*
Adjectives	*most, many, some, a certain number of*
Verbs	*may, might, can, could, seem, tend, appear, suggest, indicate*

Some readers think all hedging is not just redundant, but mealy-mouthed:

> There **seems to be some** evidence to **suggest** that **certain** differences between Japanese and Western rhetoric **could** derive from

historical influences **possibly** traceable to Japan's cultural isolation and Europe's history of cross-cultural contacts.

On the other hand, only a fool or someone with massive historical evidence would make an assertion as flatly confident as this:

This evidence **proves** that Japanese and Western rhetorics differ because of Japan's cultural isolation and Europe's history of cross-cultural contacts.

In thoughtful academic writing, we more often state claims closer to this (and look at that for my own hedging; compare the more assertive, *We state claims like this*):

✓ This evidence **suggests** that **aspects** of Japanese and Western rhetoric differ because of Japan's cultural isolation and Europe's history of cross-cultural contacts.

This next paragraph introduced the article announcing the most significant breakthrough in the history of genetics, the discovery of the double helix of DNA. If anyone was entitled to be assertive, it was Crick and Watson. But they chose to be diffident, to hedge (note, too, the first person *we;* hedges are bold-faced):

We **wish to suggest a** [note that they did not say *the*] structure for the salt of deoxyribose nucleic **acid** (D.N.A.) . . . A structure for nucleic acid has already been proposed by Pauling and Corey . . . **In our opinion,** this structure is unsatisfactory for two reasons: (1) **We believe** that the material which gives the X-ray diagrams is the salt, not the free acid . . . (2) **Some** of the van der Waals distances **appear** to be too small.

—J. D. Watson and F. H. C. Crick,
"Molecular Structure of Nucleic Acids"

Without the hedges, their claim would be more concise but more aggressive. Compare this (I boldface my stronger words, but most of the more aggressive tone comes from the absence of hedges):

We ~~wish to suggest~~ **state the** structure for the salt of deoxyribose nucleic acid (D.N.A.) . . . A structure for nucleic acid has already been proposed by Pauling and Corey . . . ~~In our opinion,~~ this structure is unsatisfactory for two reasons: (1) ~~We believe that~~ the material which gives the X-ray diagrams is the salt, not the free acid . . . (2) ~~Some of~~ the van der Waals distances ~~appear to be~~ **are** too small.

You can use the verbs *suggest* and *indicate* instead of *prove* or *show* to make a claim about which you are less than 100 percent certain, but confident enough to propose:

✓ The evidence **indicates** that some of these questions remain unresolved.

✓ These data **suggest** that further studies are necessary.

Intensifiers   These are common intensifiers:

Adverbs	*very, pretty, quite, rather, clearly, obviously, undoubtedly, certainly, of course, indeed, inevitably, invariably, always*
Adjectives	*key, central, crucial, basic, fundamental, major, principal, essential*
Verbs	*show, prove, establish, as you/we/everyone knows/can see, it is clear/obvious that*

Confident writers use intensifiers less often than they use hedges because they want to avoid sounding as smug as this:

For a century now, **all** liberals have argued against **any** censorship of art, and **every** court has found their arguments so **completely** persuasive that **not a** person **any** longer remembers how they were countered. As a result, today, censorship is **totally** a thing of the past.

Some inexperienced writers think that an aggressive style is persuasive. Quite the opposite: If you state a claim moderately, readers are more likely to consider it thoughtfully:

For **about** a century now, **many** liberals have argued against censorship of art, and **most** courts have found their arguments persuasive **enough** that **few** people **may** remember **exactly** how they were countered. As a result, today, censorship is **virtually** a thing of the past.

Some claim that a passage hedged that much is wordy and weak. Perhaps. But it does not come on like a bulldozer. It leaves room for a reasoned and equally moderate response. In fact, in some academic areas, readers assume that if you begin with *It is obvious . . .* , what you then say is not.

The most common intensifier is the absence of a hedge. In this case, less is more. The first sentence below has no intensifiers at the blanks, but neither does it have any hedges, and so it seems like a strong claim:

> _____ Americans believe that the federal government is _____ intrusive and _____ authoritarian.

> **Many** Americans believe that the federal government is **often** intrusive and **increasingly** authoritarian.

Here's the point: You need some metadiscourse in everything you write, especially metadiscourse that guides readers through your text, words such as *first, second, therefore, on the other hand,* and so on. You also need some metadiscourse that hedges your certainty, words such as *perhaps, seems, could,* and so on. The risk is that you can easily use too many.

8

Shape

The structure of every sentence is a lesson in logic.
—JOHN STUART MILL

UNDERSTANDING THE SHAPE
OF SENTENCES

Clarity in Complexity

If you can write clear and concise sentences, you have achieved a lot, and much more if you can assemble them into coherent passages. But if you can't write a clear sentence longer than twenty words or so, you're like a composer who can write only jingles. Despite those who tell us not to write long sentences, you cannot communicate every complex idea in short ones, so you have to know how to write a sentence that is both long and clear.

Consider, for example, (1a):

1a. In addition to differences in ethnicity or religion that have for centuries plagued Bosnians, Serbs, and Croats, explanations seeking causes of their hatred must include all of the other social, economic, and cultural conflicts that have plagued them that are rooted in a troubled history that extends 1000 years into the past.

Even if that idea needs all those words (it doesn't), they could be arranged in a more shapely sentence.

We can start revising by editing the abstractions into character/subjects and action/verbs and then break the sentence into shorter ones:

> 1b. Historians have tried to explain why Bosnians, Serbs, and Croats hate one another today. Many have claimed that the sources of conflict are age-old differences in ethnicity or religion. But they must study all the other social, economic, and cultural conflicts that have plagued them through their 1000 years of troubled history.

But if (1a) is shapeless, (1b) is choppy. We need something like this:

> ✓1c. To explain why Bosnians, Serbs, and Croats hate one another today, historians must study not only age-old differences of ethnicity and religion, but all the other social, economic, and cultural conflicts that have plagued them through their 1000 years of troubled history.

That sentence is long but doesn't sprawl. So it can't be length alone that makes a sentence ungainly. In this lesson, I focus on how to write sentences that are not only long and complex but clear and shapely.

DIAGNOSIS AND REVISION

It's easier to see sprawl in the writing of others than in your own because you know what you want your sentences to mean before you read them. So you have to diagnose your prose in ways that sidestep your intractable subjectivity.

Start by putting a slash mark after every period and question mark./Then pick out sentences longer than two lines and read them aloud./If in reading one of your long sentences you feel that you are about to run out of breath before you come to a place where you can pause to integrate all of its parts into a whole that communicates a single conceptual structure [breathe], you have found a sentence your readers would likely want you to revise, like this one./Or if your sentence, because of one interruption after another, seems to stop and start, your readers are, if they are typical, likely to judge that your sentence, as this one does, lurches from one part to the next.

Readers get a sense of shapeless length from three things:

- It takes them too long to get to the verb in the main clause.
- After the verb, they have to slog through a shapeless sprawl of tacked on subordinate clauses.
- They hesitate at one interruption after another.

Revising Long Openings

Some sentences seem to take forever to get to the point:

> Since most undergraduate students change their fields of study at least once during their college careers, many more than once, first-year students who are not certain about their program of studies should not load up their schedules to meet requirements for a particular program.

That sentence takes thirty-one words to get to its main verb, *should not load up.* The main claim of a sentence should usually be in the subject and verb of its main clause, so here are two rules of thumb about your sentence's beginning:

1. Get to the subject of the main clause quickly; avoid beginning more than a few sentences with long introductory phrases and clauses.
2. Get to the verb and object of the main clause quickly; avoid long, abstract subjects and interruptions between subjects and verbs and between verbs and their objects.

Rule of Thumb 1: Get to the Subject Quickly We have a problem with sentences that open with long introductory phrases and clauses, because as we read them, we have to hold in mind that the subject and verb of the main clause are still to come, and that frustrates easy understanding.

Compare these next examples. As we read the first seventeen words in (2a), we have to hold in mind that a subject of a main clause is coming.

2a. **Since most undergraduate students change their major fields of study at least once during their college careers,** *first-year students* who are not certain about the program of studies they want to pursue SHOULD NOT LOAD UP their schedules to meet requirements for a particular program.

In (2b), we get past the subjects and verbs of the first two clauses in just a few words.

✓2b. **Most undergraduate students** CHANGE their major fields at least once during their college careers, so **first-year students** SHOULD NOT LOAD UP their schedules with requirements for a particular program if they are not certain about the program of studies they want to pursue.

If you open with a long introductory clause, try moving it to the end of its sentence or turning it into a sentence of its own.

Rule of Thumb 2: Get to the Verb and Object Quickly
Readers also want to get past the main subject to its verb and object. Therefore,

- keep subjects short,
- avoid interrupting the subject-verb connection,
- avoid interrupting the verb-object connection.

There are two ways to shorten subjects.

Revise Long Subjects into Short Ones   Start by underlining your WHOLE SUBJECTS. If you find a long subject (more than seven or eight words) including nominalizations, try turning the nominalization into a verb and finding a subject for it (review pp. 26–27):

Abco Inc.'s *understanding* of the drivers of its profitability in the Asian market for small electronics helped it pursue opportunities in Africa.

✓ **Abco Inc.** was able to pursue opportunities in Africa because it understood what drove profitability in the Asian market for small electronics.

A subject can also be long if it includes a long relative clause:

> A company **that focuses on hiring the best personnel and then trains them not just for the work they are hired to do but for higher-level jobs** is likely to earn the loyalty of its employees.

Try turning the relative clause into an introductory subordinate clause:

> ✓ **When a company focuses on hiring the best personnel and then trains them not just for the work they are hired to do but for higher-level jobs,** it is likely to earn the loyalty of its employees.

But if the introductory clause turns out to be as long as that one, move it to the end of its sentence, especially if the main clause is short and to the point and the moveable clause expresses newer and more complex information.

> ✓ A company is likely to earn the loyalty of its employees **when** it focuses on hiring the best personnel and then trains them not just for the work they are hired to do but for higher-level jobs.

Or turn it into a sentence of its own.

> ✓ Some companies focus on hiring the best personnel and then train them not just for the work they are hired to do but for higher-level jobs later. **Such companies are likely to earn the loyalty of their employees.**

Avoid Interrupting the Subject-Verb Connection   You also frustrate readers when you interrupt the connection between a subject and verb, like this:

> Some scientists, **because they write in a style that is impersonal and objective,** do not easily communicate with laypeople.

That *because*-clause after the subject forces us to hold our mental breath until we reach the verb, *do not easily communicate.* Move the interruption to the beginning or end of its sentence, depending on whether it connects more closely to what came before or comes after. (Review pp. 54–56.):

✓ Because some scientists write in a style that is impersonal and objective, they do **not easily communicate with laypeople. This lack of communication** damages . . .

✓ Some scientists do not easily communicate with laypeople because they write in **a style that is impersonal and objective. It is a kind of style** filled with passives and . . .

We mind short interruptions less:

✓ Some scientists **deliberately** write in a style that is impersonal and objective.

Avoid Interrupting the Verb-Object Connection   We also like to get past the verb to its object quickly. This sentence doesn't let us do that:

> We must develop, **if we are to become competitive with other companies in our region,** a core of knowledge regarding the state of the art in effective industrial organizations.

Move the interrupting element to the beginning or end of its sentence, depending on what comes next:

✓ **If we are to compete with other companies in our region,** we must develop a core of knowledge about the state of the art in **effective industrial organizations. Such organizations provide . . .**

✓ **We** must develop a core of knowledge about the state of the art in effective industrial organizations **if we are to compete with other companies in our region. Increasing competition . . .**

There is an exception to that advice. When a prepositional phrase you can move is shorter than a long object, try putting the phrase between the verb and object:

> In a long sentence, put the newest and most important information that you want your reader to remember **at its end.**

✓ In a long sentence, put **at its end** the newest and most important information that you want your reader to remember.

This is an example of a very general principle that governs more than style: arrange elements in a sentence from short to long, from simple to complex.

> ***Here's the point:***   Readers read most easily when you quickly get them
> - to the subject of your main clause and
> - past that subject to its verb and object.
>
> Avoid long introductory phrases and clauses, long subjects, and interruptions between subjects and verbs, and between verbs and objects.

Reshaping Sprawl

Once readers make the subject-verb-object connection, they can deal with longer, more complex chunks of information that follow. But they don't want to slog through sprawl like this:

> Of the many areas of science important to our future, few are more promising than genetic engineering, which is a new way of manipulating the elemental structural units of life itself, which are the genes and chromosomes that tell our cells how to reproduce to become the parts that constitute our bodies.

A sentence sprawls when after the verb and object, it tacks on a series of subordinate clauses of the same kind. It looks like this:

> Of the many areas of science important to our future,
>   *[opening phrase]*
>
>   few are more promising than genetic engineering,
>   *[subject-verb core]*
>
>   **which** is a new way of manipulating the elemental structural units of life itself, *[tacked-on relative clause]*
>
>   **which** are the genes and chromosomes
>   *[tacked-on relative clause]*
>
>   **that** tell our cells how to reproduce to become the parts
>   [tacked-on relative clause]
>
>   **that** constitute our bodies.
>   *[tacked-on relative clause]*

Diagnose this problem by having someone read your prose aloud. If that reader gets confused or runs out of breath before getting to the end of a sentence, so will your silent reader. You can revise in three ways:

1. Cut

1. Try reducing some of the relative clauses to phrases by deleting *who/that/which* + *is/was,* etc.:

   ✓ Of the many areas of science important to our future, few are more promising than genetic engineering, ~~which is~~ a new way of manipulating the elemental structural units of life itself, ~~which are~~ the genes and chromosomes that tell our cells how to reproduce to become the parts that constitute our bodies.

   Occasionally, you have to rewrite the remaining verb into an *-ing* form:

   The day is coming when we will all have numbers **that will identify** our financial transactions so that the IRS can monitor all activities **that involve** economic activity.

   ✓ The day is coming when we will all have numbers ~~that will~~ **identifying** our financial transactions so that the IRS can monitor all activities ~~that~~ **involving** economic activity.

2. Or break the subordinate clauses out into their own sentences.

   ✓ Many areas of science are important to our future, but few are more promising than genetic engineering. It is a new way of manipulating the elemental structural units of life itself, the genes and chromosomes that tell our cells how to reproduce to become the parts that constitute our bodies.

   If none of that works, you have to do some major restructuring.

2. Change Clauses to Modifying Phrases   You can write a long sentence but still avoid sprawl if you change relative clauses to one of three kinds of modifying phrases: resumptive, summative, or free. You have probably never read those terms before, but they refer to stylistic devices you should know how to use.

Resumptive Modifiers   These two examples contrast a relative clause and a resumptive modifier:

> Since mature writers often use resumptive modifiers to extend a sentence, we need a word to name what I have not done in this sentence, **which I could have ended after the word** *sentence* **but extended to show you a relative clause attached to a noun.**

> ✓ Since mature writers often use resumptive modifiers to extend a sentence, we need a word to name what I am about to do in this sentence, **a sentence that I could have ended at that comma, but extended to show you how resumptive modifiers work.**

The boldface resumptive modifier repeats a key word and starts again.

To create a resumptive modifier, find a key noun just before the tacked on clause, then pause after it with a comma:

> Since mature writers often use resumptive modifiers to extend a sentence, we need a word to name what I am about to do in this **sentence,**

Then repeat the noun:

> Since mature writers often use resumptive modifiers to extend a sentence, we need a word to name what I am about to do in this **sentence,**
>
> **a sentence . . .**

Then to that repeated word add a relative clause beginning with *that:*

> Since mature writers often use resumptive modifiers to extend a sentence, we need a word to name what I am about to do in this sentence,
>
> a sentence **that I could have ended at that comma, but extended to show you how resumptive modifiers work.**

You can also resume with an adjective or verb. In that case, you don't add a relative clause; you just repeat the adjective or verb and continue.

✓ It was American writers who found a voice that was both **true** and **lyrical,**

> **true** to the rhythms of the working man's speech and **lyrical** in its celebration of his labor.

✓ All who value independence should **resist** the trivialization of government regulation,

> **resist** its obsession with administrative tidiness and compulsion to arrange things not for our convenience but for theirs.

Summative Modifiers   Here are two sentences that contrast relative clauses and summative modifiers. Notice how the *which* in the first one feels "tacked on":

> Economic changes have reduced Russian population growth to less than zero, **which will have serious social implications.**

✓ Economic changes have reduced Russian population growth to less than zero, **a demographic event that will have serious social implications.**

To create a summative modifier, end a grammatically complete segment of a sentence with a comma:

> Economic changes have reduced Russian population growth to less than zero,

Find a term that sums up the substance of the sentence:

> Economic changes have reduced Russian population growth to less than zero,
>
> **a demographic event . . .**

Then continue with a relative clause beginning with *that:*

> Economic changes have reduced Russian population growth to less than zero,
>
> a demographic event **that will have serious social implications.**

Free Modifiers   Like the other modifiers, a free modifier can appear at the end of a clause, but instead of repeating a key word or summing up what went before, it says something about the subject of the closest verb:

✓ Free modifiers resemble resumptive and summative modifiers, **letting you** [i.e., the free modifier lets you] **extend the line of a sentence while avoiding a train of ungainly phrases and clauses.**

Free modifiers usually begin with an *-ing* present participle, as those did, but they can also begin with a past participle verb, like this:

✓ Leonardo da Vinci was a man of powerful intellect,

> *driven* **by** [i.e., Leonardo was driven by] **an insatiable curiosity and** *haunted* **by a vision of artistic perfection.**

A free modifier can also begin with an adjective:

✓ In 1939, we began to assist the British against Germany,

> *aware* [i.e., we were aware] **that we faced another world war.**

We call these modifiers "free" because they can both begin and end a sentence:

✓ **Driven by an insatiable curiosity,** Leonardo da Vinci was . . .

✓ **Aware that we faced another world war,** in 1939 we began . . .

Create a free modifier, however, and you risk dangling it. A modifier "dangles" when its implied subject differs from the explicit subject of the clause it attaches to:

Hoping to find the flaw, the results of the tests were reviewed.

The modifier, *hoping to find,* dangles because its implicit subject (whoever hopes) differs from the explicit subject of the clause it attaches to (*the results of the tests*). To revise, make the implied and explicit subjects the same:

✓ **Hoping** to find the flaw, **we** reviewed the results of the tests.

Most readers ignore a dangling modifier when it is metadiscourse.

✓ **To summarize,** it is clear that . . .

✓ **Turning to our finances,** our first question is . . .

Here's the point: When you have to write a long sentence, don't just add one phrase or clause after another, willy-nilly. Particularly avoid tacking one relative clause onto another onto another. Try extending the line of a sentence with resumptive, summative, and free modifiers. When you create a free modifier, however, be sure its implied subject matches the explicit subject of the verb closest to it.

---

3. Coordinate It's harder to create good coordination than good modifiers, but when done well, it's more pleasing to the reader. Coordination is in fact the foundation of a gracefully shaped sentence. Compare these. My version is first; the original is second:

> The aspiring artist may find that even a minor, unfinished work which was botched may be an instructive model for how things should be done, while for the amateur spectator, such works are the daily fare which may provide good, honest nourishment, which can lead to an appreciation of deeper pleasures that are also more refined.

✓ For the aspiring artist, the minor, the unfinished, or even the botched work, may be an instructive model for how things should—and should not—be done. For the amateur spectator, such works are the daily fare which provide good, honest nourishment—and which can lead to appreciation of more refined, or deeper pleasures.

> —Eva Hoffman, "Minor Art Offers Special Pleasures"

My revision sprawls through a string of tacked-on clauses:

> The aspiring artist may find that even a minor, unfinished work
> **which** was botched may be an instructive model for
> **how** things should be done,
> **while** for the amateur spectator, such works are the daily fare
> **which** may provide good, honest nourishment,

> **which** can lead to an appreciation of deeper pleasures
>   **that** are also more refined.

Hoffman's original gets its shape from its multiple coordinations. Structurally, it looks like this:

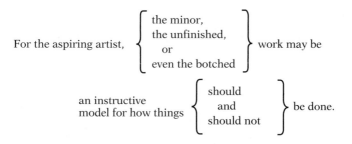

For the amateur spectator, such works are

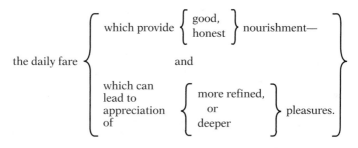

That second sentence in particular shows how elaborate coordination can get.

A General Design Principle: Short to Long   We should note one feature that distinguishes well-formed coordination. You can hear it if you read this next passage aloud:

> We should devote a few final words to a matter that reaches beyond the techniques of research to the connections between those subjective values that reflect our deepest ethical choices and objective research.

That sentence seems to end too abruptly with *objective research*. Structurally, it looks like this:

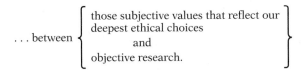

This next revision moves from shorter to longer by reversing the two coordinate elements and by adding a parallelism to the second one to make it longer. Read this one aloud:

> We should devote a few final words to a matter that reaches beyond the techniques of research to the connections between objective research and those subjective values that reflect our deepest ethical choices and strongest intellectual commitments.

Structurally, it looks like this:

$$
✔ \ldots \text{between} \left\{ \begin{array}{l} \text{objective research} \\ \text{and} \\ \text{those subjective} \\ \text{values that reflect our} \end{array} \left\{ \begin{array}{l} \text{deepest ethical choices} \\ \text{and} \\ \text{strongest intellectual} \\ \text{commitments.} \end{array} \right. \right\}
$$

Here's the point: Coordination lets you extend the line of a sentence more gracefully than just by tacking on one element to another. When you can coordinate, try to order the elements so that they go from shorter to longer, from simpler to more complex.

Troubleshooting Long Sentences

Even when you manage their internal structures, though, long sentences can still go wrong.

Faulty Coordination   Ordinarily, we coordinate elements only of the same grammatical structure: clause and clause, prepositional phrase and prepositional phrase, and so on. When you coordinate different grammatical structures, readers may feel you have created an offensive lack of parallelism. Careful writers avoid this:

The committee recommends
{
revising the curriculum to recognize trends in local employment
and
that the division be reorganized to reflect the new curriculum.
}

They would correct that to this:

✔ . . . recommends
{
that the curriculum be revised to recognize . . .
and
that the division be reorganized to reflect. . . .
}

Or to this:

✔ . . . recommends
{
revising the curriculum to recognize . . .
and
reorganizing the division to reflect. . . .
}

However, some nonparallel coordinations do occur in well-written prose. Careful writers coordinate a noun phrase with a *how*-clause:

✔ We will attempt to delineate
{
the problems of education in developing nations
and
how coordinated efforts can address them in economical ways.
}

Or they coordinate an adverb with a prepositional phrase:

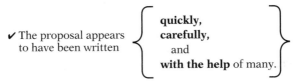

✔ The proposal appears
   to have been written

quickly,
carefully,
   and
with the help of many.

Careful readers do not blink at either.

We respond to coordination best when the elements are coordinate not only in grammar but in thought. Some inexperienced writers coordinate by just joining one element to another with *and:*

> Grade inflation is a problem at many universities, ***and*** it leads to a devaluation of good grades earned by hard work ***and*** will not be solved simply by grading harder.

Those *and*s obscure the relationships among those claims:

> ✓ Grade inflation is a problem at many universities, **because** it devalues good grades that were earned by hard work, **but** it will not be solved simply by grading harder.

Unfortunately, I can't tell you how to recognize when elements are not coordinate in thought.

Unclear Connections   Readers are also bothered by a coordination so long that they lose track of its internal connections and pronoun references:

> Teachers should remember that students are vulnerable and uncertain about those everyday ego-bruising moments that adults ignore and that they do not understand that one day they will become as confident and as secure as the adults that bruise them.

We sense a flicker of hesitation about where to connect:

> . . . and that they do not understand that one day they . . .

To revise a sentence like that, shorten the first half of the coordination so that you can start the second half closer to the point where the coordination began:

✓ Teachers should remember that students are vulnerable to ego-bruising moments that adults ignore and that they do not understand that one day . . .

If you can't do that, repeat a word that reminds the reader where the coordination began (thereby creating a resumptive modifier):

✓ Teachers should try to remember that students are vulnerable to ego-bruising moments that adults ignore, **to remember** that they do not understand that . . .

Misplaced Modifiers   Another problem with modifiers is that sometimes readers are unsure what they modify:

Overtaxing oneself in physical activity too frequently results in injury.

What happens too frequently, overtaxing or injuries? We can make its meaning unambiguous by moving *too frequently:*

✓ Overtaxing oneself too frequently in physical activity results in injury.
✓ Overtaxing oneself in physical activity results too frequently in injury.

A modifier at the end of a clause can ambiguously modify either a neighboring or a more distant phrase:

Scientists have learned that their observations are as subjective as those in any other field **in recent years.**

We can move the modifier to a less ambiguous position:

✓ **In recent years,** scientists have learned that . . .
✓ Scientists have learned that **in recent years** their . . .

Here's the point: Even well-constructed long sentences can give readers a problem if they can't connect the second part of a coordination to its starting point or if they are unsure about what a phrase actually modifies.

Intrinsic Sense

You can use these devices to shape a long yet clear sentence, but not even the best syntax can salvage incoherent ideas. This next sentence appeared in a Sunday *New York Times* travel section. The sentence before it had introduced the professional women of Amsterdam's red-light district:

> They are so unself-conscious about their profession that by day they can be seen standing naked in doorways, chatting with their neighbors in the shadow of the Oudekerstoren Church, which offers Saturday carillon concerts at 4 P.M. and a panoramic view of the city from its tower in summer.

This syntactically well-formed sentence opens with a coherent clause:

> They are so unself-conscious about their profession that by day they can be seen standing naked in doorways . . .

It continues with a free modifier:

> . . . chatting with their neighbors in the shadow of the Oudekerstoren Church . . .

then concludes with a relative clause with a balanced pair of direct objects:

. . . which offers
{
Saturday carillon concerts at 4 P.M.
and
a panoramic view of the city from its tower in summer.
}

But the movement of ideas is goofy (or evidence of a sly sense of humor).

9

Elegance

Anything is better than not to write clearly.
There is nothing to be said against lucidity,
and against simplicity only the possibility of dryness.
This is a risk well worth taking when you reflect
how much better it is to be bald
than to wear a curly wig.
—SOMERSET MAUGHAM

UNDERSTANDING ELEGANCE

Anyone who can write clearly, concisely, and coherently should rejoice to achieve so much. But while most of us prefer bald clarity to the density of institutional prose, others feel that relentless simplicity can be dry, even arid. It has the spartan virtue of unsalted meat and potatoes, but such fare is rarely memorable. A flash of elegance can not only fix a thought in our minds, but give us a flicker of pleasure every time we recall it. This lesson is for those of you who aim at prose that is more than just clear and coherent, that offers a moment of pleasure not just for your reader but for yourself.

Unfortunately, I can't tell you how to do that. In fact, I incline toward those who think that the most elegant elegance is disarming simplicity—and so when you think you have written something fine, I second some old advice: strike it out. Never-theless, there are a few devices that can shape a thought in ways that are both elegant and clear.

Just knowing them, however, is about as useful as just knowing the ingredients in the bouillabaisse of a great cook, and then thinking you can make it. Knowing ingredients and knowing how to use them distinguish reading cookbooks and cooking. Maybe elegant clarity is a gift. But even a gift has to be educated and exercised.

Balance and Symmetry

What most makes a sentence graceful is a balance and symmetry among its parts, one echoing another in sound, rhythm, struc-ture, and meaning. A skilled writer can balance almost any two parts of a sentence, but the most common balance is based on coordination.

Balanced Coordination   Here is a balanced passage and my revision of it. A tin ear can distinguish which is which:

1a. The national unity of a free people depends upon a sufficiently even balance of political power to make it impracticable for the administration to be arbitrary and for the opposition to be revolutionary and irreconcilable. Where that balance no longer exists, democracy perishes. For unless all the citizens of a state are forced by circumstances to compromise, unless they feel that they can affect policy but that no one can wholly dominate it, unless by habit and necessity they have to give and take, free-dom cannot be maintained.

—Walter Lippmann

1b. The national unity of a free people depends upon a sufficiently even balance of political power to make it impracticable for an administration to be arbitrary against a revolutionary oppo-sition that is irreconcilably opposed to it. Where that balance no longer exists, democracy perishes, because unless all the

> citizens of a state are habitually forced by necessary circumstances to compromise in a way that lets them affect policy with no one dominating it, freedom cannot be maintained.

My sentences lurch from one part to the next. In Lippmann's, we hear one clause and phrase echo another in word order, sound, and meaning, giving the whole passage an intricate architectural symmetry.

If we extend the idea of topic and stress from a whole sentence to its parts, we can see how he balances even short segments. Note how each significant word in one phrase echoes another in its corresponding one (I boldface topics of phrases and italicize stresses):

> The national unity of a free people depends upon a sufficiently even balance of political power to make it impracticable

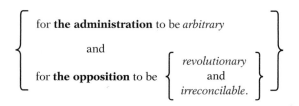

Lippmann balances the phrasal topics of *administration* and *opposition,* and closes by balancing the stressed sounds and meanings of *arbitrary, revolutionary,* and *irreconcilable.* He follows with a short concluding sentence whose stressed words are not coordinated, but are still balanced (I use square brackets to indicate noncoordinated balance):

> Where [**that balance** *no longer exists,* **democracy** *perishes.*]

Then he creates an especially intricate design, balancing many sounds and meanings:

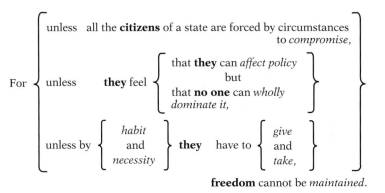

freedom cannot be *maintained*.

- He repeats *citizens* as the subject/topic of each clause: *all the citizens, they, they* (note the passive in the first one: *citizens are forced*).
- He balances the sound and sense of *force* against *feel*, and the meaning of *affect policy* against the meaning of *dominate it*.
- In the last *unless*-clause, he balances the meaning of *habit* against *necessity*, and the stressed *give* against *take*.
- He balances the meanings of *compromise, affect, dominate*, and *give and take*.
- Then to balance the clauses of that short preceding sentence, *balance no longer exists—democracy perishes*, he concludes with an equally short clause, *freedom cannot be maintained*, whose meaning and structure echo the corresponding pair in the preceding sentence:

balance	no longer exists
democracy	perishes
freedom	cannot be maintained

For those who care and notice, it is an impressive construction.

Uncoordinated Balance   We can also balance structures that are not grammatically coordinate. In this example, the subject balances the object:

> **Scientists** whose research   *creates revolutionary views of*
> *the universe*
>
>   invariably upset
>
> **those of us** who   *construct our vision of reality*
> *out of our common-sense experience*
> *of it.*

Here, the predicate of a relative clause in a subject balances the predicate of the sentence:

> A government
> > that is unwilling to *listen* to   the *moderate hopes* of *its citizenry*
> >
> > must eventually   *answer* to the *harsh justice* of *its revolutionaries.*

Here a direct object balances the object of a preposition:

Those of us concerned with our school systems will not sacrifice

> the *intellectual growth* of   our *innocent children*
>   to
> the *social engineering* of   *incompetent bureaucrats.*

A more complicated balance:

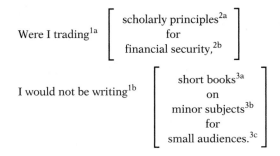

In that sentence,

- a subordinate clause (1a), *Were I trading,* balances the main clause (1b), *I would not be writing;*
- the object of that subordinate clause (2a), *scholarly principles,* balances the object in the prepositional phrase (2b), *financial security;*
- the object in the main clause (3a), *short books,* balances the objects in two prepositional phrases, (3b), *minor subjects,* and (3c), *small audiences* (and note the balance of *short, minor,* and *small*).

Keep in mind that you usually create the most rhythmical balance when the first element in a balance is shorter than the next ones (see p. 100).

Used to excess, these patterns can seem merely clever, but used prudently, they can emphasize an important point or conclude a line of reasoning with a flourish that careful readers notice.

These patterns even encourage you to think in ways that you might not have otherwise. In that sense, these patterns don't just frame thinking; they generate it. Suppose you begin a sentence like this:

> In his earliest years, Picasso was a master draftsman of the traditional human form.

Now try this:

> In his earliest years, Picasso was **not only** a master draftsman of the traditional human form, **but also** . . .

Now you have to wonder what else he might have been. Or not have been.

Here's the point: The most striking feature of elegant prose is balanced sentence structures. You most easily balance one part of a sentence against another by coordinating them with *and, or, nor, but,* and *yet,* but you can also balance noncoordinated phrases and clauses.

Climactic Emphasis

How you begin a sentence determines its clarity; how you end it determines its rhythm and grace.

Light and Heavy Words   When we get close to the end of a sentence, we expect words that deserve stress (p. 68), so we may feel a sentence is anticlimactic if it ends on words of slight grammatical or semantic weight. At the end of a sentence, prepositions feel light—one reason we sometimes avoid leaving one there. The rhythm of a sentence should carry readers toward strength. Compare:

> Studies into intellectual differences among races is a project that only the most politically naive psychologist is willing to give support to.

> ✓ Studies into intellectual differences among races is a project that only the most politically naive scientist is willing to support.

Adjectives and adverbs are heavier than prepositions, but lighter than nouns, the heaviest of which are nominalizations. Readers have problems with nominalizations in the subject of a sentence, but at the end they provide a satisfyingly climactic thump, particularly when two of them are in coordinate balance. Consider this excerpt from Winston Churchill's "Finest Hour" speech. Churchill ended it with a parallelism climaxed by a balanced pair of heavy nominalizations:

. . . until in God's good time,

the New World, with all its $\left\{ \begin{array}{c} \text{power} \\ \text{and} \\ \text{might} \end{array} \right\}$ steps forth to

$\left\{ \begin{array}{c} \text{the \textbf{rescue}} \\ \text{and} \\ \text{the \textbf{liberation}} \end{array} \right\}$ of the old.

He could have written more simply, and more banally:

. . . until the New World rescues us.

Elegant Stress: Three Devices   Here are three ways to end a sentence with special emphasis.

1. *of* + **Nominalization.** This seems unlikely, but it's true. Look at how Churchill ends his sentence: The light *of* (followed by a lighter *a* or *the*) quickens the rhythm of a sentence just before the stress of the climactic monosyllable, *old:*

   . . . the rescue and the liberation of the **old.**

   We associate this pattern with self-conscious elegance, as in the first few sentences of Edward Gibbon's *History of the Decline and Fall of the Roman Empire* (contrast that title with *The Roman Empire's Fall*):

✓ In the second century of the Christian era, the Empire of Rome comprehended **the fairest part** *of* **the earth,** AND **the most civilized portion** *of* **mankind.** The frontiers of that extensive monarchy were guarded **by ancient renown** AND **disciplined valour.** The gentle but powerful influence of laws and manners had gradually cemented **the union** *of* **the provinces.** Their peaceful inhabitants **enjoyed** AND **abused the advantages** *of* **wealth** AND **luxury.** The image of a free constitution was preserved with decent **reverence:** the Roman senate appeared to possess the sovereign authority, and devolved on the emperors all **the executive powers** *of* **government.**

In comparison, this is flat:

In the second century AD, the Roman Empire comprehended **the earth's fairest, most civilized part.** Ancient renown and disciplined valour guarded **its extensive frontiers.** The gentle but powerful influence of laws and manners had gradually **unified the provinces.** Their peaceful inhabitants enjoyed and abused luxurious wealth while decently preserving what seemed to be **a free constitution.** Appearing to possess the sovereign authority, the Roman senate devolved on the emperors all **executive governmental powers.**

2. **Echoing Salience.** At the end of a sentence, readers hear special emphasis when a stressed word or phrase balances the sound or meaning of an earlier one. (These examples are all from Peter Gay's *Style in History*.)

✓ I have written these essays to anatomize this familiar yet really strange being, **style the centaur;** the book may be read as an extended critical commentary on Buffon's famous saying that **the style is the man.**

When we hear a stressed word echo an earlier one, these balances become even more emphatic:

✓ Apart from a few mechanical tricks of rhetoric, **manner** is indissolubly linked to **matter; style shapes,** and in turn is **shaped** by, **substance.**

✓ It seems frivolous, almost inappropriate, to be **stylish** about **style.**

Gay echoes both the sound and meaning of *manner* in *matter, style* in *substance, shapes* in *shaped by,* and *stylish* in *style.*

3. **Chiasmus.** This device (pronounced kye-ᴀᴢᴢ-muss,) is interesting perhaps only to those fascinated with the most obscure figures of style. The word *chiasmus* is from the Greek word for "crossing." It balances elements in two parts of a sentence, but the second part reverses the order of the elements in the first part. For example, this would be both coordinate and parallel, but not a chiasmus, because the elements in the two parts are in the same order (AB : AB):

✔ A concise style
  can improve both

$$\left\{ \begin{array}{c} \text{\textbf{our own}}^{1A} \ \textit{thinking}^{1B} \\ \text{and} \\ \text{\textbf{our readers'}}^{2A} \ \textit{understanding.}^{2B} \end{array} \right\}$$

Were we seeking a special effect, we could reverse the order of elements in the second part to mirror those in the first. Now the pattern is not 1A1B : 2A2B, but rather 1A1B : 2B2A:

✔ A concise style
  can improve not only

$$\left\{ \begin{array}{c} \text{\textbf{our own}}^{1A} \ \textit{thinking}^{1B} \\ \text{but} \\ \text{the } \textit{understanding}^{2B} \text{ \textbf{of our readers.}}^{2A} \end{array} \right\}$$

The next example is more complex. The first two elements are parallel, but the last three mirror one another: AB CDE : AB EDC:

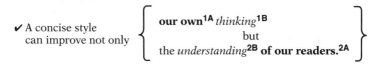

$$\left[\begin{array}{l} \text{You}^{A} \quad \text{reveal}^{B} \quad \text{\textbf{your own}}^{C} \ \textit{highest rhetorical}^{D} \ \textsc{skill}^{E} \\ \qquad\qquad \text{by the way} \\ \text{you}^{A} \quad \text{respect}^{B} \ \textsc{the beliefs}^{E} \ \textit{most deeply held}^{D} \ \text{\textbf{by your reader.}}^{C} \end{array} \right]$$

> ***Here's the point:***   An elegant sentence should end on strength. You can create that strength in four ways:
>
> 1. End with a strong word, typically a nominalization, or better, a pair of them.
> 2. End with a prepositional phrase introduced by *of*.
> 3. End with an echoing salience.
> 4. End with a chiasmus.

Extravagant Elegance

When writers combine all these elements in a single sentence, we know they are aiming at something special, as in this next passage by Joyce Carol Oates:

> Far from being locked inside our own skins, inside the "dungeons" of ourselves, we are now able to recognize that our minds belong, quite naturally, to a collective "mind," a mind in which we share everything that is mental, most obviously language itself, and that the old boundary of the skin is not boundary at all but a membrane connecting the inner and outer experience of existence. Our intelligence, our wit, our cleverness, our unique personalities—all are simultaneously "our own" possessions and the world's.
>
> —Joyce Carol Oates, "New Heaven and New Earth"

Here is the anatomy of that passage:

Far from being locked **inside** our own skins,

        inside the "dungeons" of ourselves,

we are now able to recognize

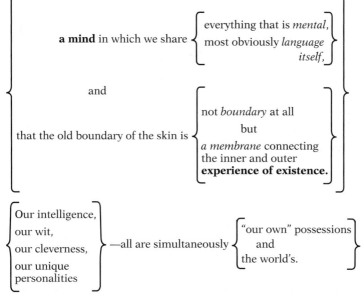

In addition to all the coordination, note the two resumptive modifiers:

    Far from being locked **inside** our own skins,
              inside the "dungeons" of ourselves . . .

    our minds belong . . . to a collective **"mind,"**
              a mind in which we share . . .

Note too the two nominalizations stressed at the end of the first sentence and the coordinate nominalizations ending the second:

> . . . the inner and outer experience of existence.

> . . . "our own" possessions and the world's.

But such patterns can be more elaborate yet. Here is the last sentence from Frederick Jackson Turner's *The Frontier in American History:*

> This then is the heritage of the pioneer experience—a passionate belief that a democracy was possible which should leave the individual a part to play in a free society and not make him a cog in a machine operated from above; which trusted in the common man, in his tolerance, his ability to adjust differences with good humor, and to work out an American type from the contributions of all nations—a type for which he would fight against those who challenged it in arms, and for which in time of war he would make sacrifices, even the temporary sacrifice of his individual freedom and his life, lest that freedom be lost forever.

Note the following:

- the summative modifier in the opening segment: *a passionate belief in* . . . ;
- the increased length and weight of the second element in each coordination, even the coordinations inside coordinations;
- the two resumptive modifiers beginning with *type* and *sacrifice.*

That may be over the top, especially the quadruple chiasmus in the last sixteen words:

the temporary[1]   sacrifice[2]   of his individual FREEDOM[3] and *his life*[4],

lest[4]   that FREEDOM[3] be   lost[2]   **forever**[1].

The meaning of *temporary* balances *forever; sacrifice* balances *lost; freedom* echoes *freedom;* and the sound of *life* balances *lest* (not to mention the near rhyme of *lest* in *lost*). You just don't see that kind of sentence any more.

Here is the anatomy of that sentence:

This then is the heritage of the pioneer experience—
[summative modifier]   a passionate belief that a democracy was possible

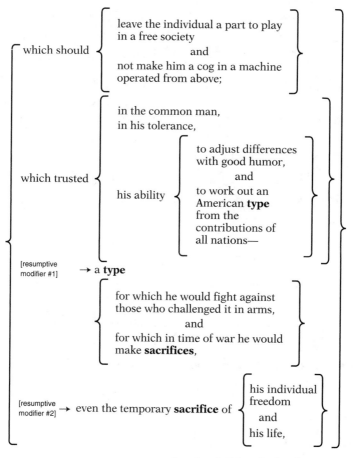

which should   leave the individual a part to play in a free society
and
not make him a cog in a machine operated from above;

which trusted   in the common man, in his tolerance,
his ability   to adjust differences with good humor, and
to work out an American **type** from the contributions of all nations—

[resumptive modifier #1]   → a **type**

for which he would fight against those who challenged it in arms, and
for which in time of war he would make **sacrifices**,

[resumptive modifier #2]   → even the temporary **sacrifice** of   his individual freedom
and
his life,

lest that freedom be lost forever.

Nuances of Length and Rhythm

Most writers don't plan the length of their sentences, but that's not a problem, unless every sentence is shorter than fifteen or so words, or much longer. Artful writers, however, do use the length of a sentence for a purpose. Some write short sentences to strike a note of urgency:

> Toward noon Petrograd again became the field of military action; rifles and machine guns rang out everywhere. It was not easy to tell who was shooting or where. One thing was clear; the past and the future were exchanging shots. There was much casual firing; young boys were shooting off revolvers unexpectedly acquired. The arsenal was wrecked. . . . Shots rang out on both sides. But the board fence stood in the way, dividing the soldiers from the revolution. The attackers decided to break down the fence. They broke down part of it and set fire to the rest. About twenty barracks came into view. The bicyclists were concentrated in two or three of them. The empty barracks were set fire to at once.
>
> —Leon Trotsky, *The Russian Revolution,* trans. Max Eastman

Or terse certainty:

> The teacher or lecturer is a danger. He very seldom recognizes his nature or his position. The lecturer is a man who must talk for an hour. France may possibly have acquired the intellectual leadership of Europe when their academic period was cut down to 40 minutes. I also have lectured. The lecturer's first problem is to have enough words to fill 40 or 60 minutes. The professor is paid for his time, his results are almost impossible to estimate . . . No teacher has ever failed from ignorance. That is empiric professional knowledge. Teachers fail because they cannot "handle the class." Real education must ultimately be limited to men who INSIST on knowing, the rest is mere sheep-herding.
>
> —Ezra Pound, *ABC of Reading*

Or passion. Here, D. H. Lawrence breaks what could have been a long paragraph into urgent utterances.

> Let us look at this American artist first. How did he ever get to America, to start with? Why isn't he a European still, like his father before him?

Now listen to me, don't listen to him. He'll tell you the lie you expect. Which is partly your fault for expecting it.

He didn't come in search of freedom of worship. England had more freedom of worship in the year 1700 than America had. Won by Englishmen who wanted freedom and so stopped at home and fought for it. And got it. Freedom of worship? Read the history of New England during the first century of its existence.

Freedom anyhow? The land of the free! This the land of the free! Why, if I say anything that displeases them, the free mob will lynch me, and that's my freedom. Free? Why I have never been in any country where the individual has such an abject fear of his fellow countrymen. Because, as I say, they are free to lynch him the moment he shows he is not one of them. . . .

All right then, what did they come for? For lots of reasons. Perhaps least of all in search of freedom of any sort: positive freedom, that is.

—D. H. Lawrence, *Studies in Classic American Literature*

Self-conscious stylists also write extravagantly long sentences. Here is just a piece of one whose sinuous length seems to mirror the confused progress of a protest march:

In any event, up at the front of this March, in the first line, back of that hollow square of monitors, Mailer and Lowell walked in this barrage of cameras, helicopters, TV cars, monitors, loudspeakers, and wavering buckling twisting line of notables, arms linked (line twisting so much that at times the movement was in file, one arm locked ahead, one behind, then the line would undulate about and the other arm would be ahead) speeding up a few steps, slowing down while a great happiness came back into the day as if finally one stood under some mythical arch in the great vault of history, helicopters buzzing about, chop-chop, and the sense of America divided on this day now liberated some undiscovered patriotism in Mailer so that he felt a sharp searing love for his country in this moment and on this day, crossing some divide in his own mind wider than the Potomac, a love so lacerated he felt as if a marriage were being torn and children lost—never does one love so much as then, obviously, then—and an odor of wood smoke, from where you knew not, was also in the air, a smoke of dignity and some calm heroism, not unlike the sense of freedom which also comes when a marriage is burst—Mailer knew for the first time why men in the front line of battle are almost always ready to die; there is a promise of some swift transit . . . [it goes on]

—Norman Mailer, *The Armies of the Night*

We almost feel we are eavesdropping on Mailer's stream of thought. But of course, such a sentence is the product not of a spontaneous moment but of premeditated art.

- Mailer opens with short, staccato phrases to suggest confusion, but he controls them by coordination.
- He continues the sentence by coordinating free modifiers: *arms linked . . . (line twisting . . .) speeding up . . .*
- After several more free modifiers, he continues with a resumptive modifier: *a love so lacerated . . .*
- After another grammatical sentence, he adds another resumptive modifier: *a smoke of dignity and some calm heroism . . .*

Here's the point: Think about the length of your sentences only if they are all longer than thirty words or so or shorter than fifteen. Your sentences will vary naturally if you simply edit them in the ways you've seen here. But if the occasion allows, don't be reluctant to experiment.

You won't acquire an elegant style just by reading this book. You must also read enough writers who write elegantly until their style runs along your muscles and nerves. Only then can you look at your own prose and know when it is elegant or just inflated. To make that distinction, I think the only reliable rule is "Less is more." Of the many graces of style, the compression of a snail is still, I think, the first.

The Ethics of Style

*Ethics is in origin the art of recommending to others
the sacrifices required for cooperation with oneself.*
—BERTRAND RUSSELL

Style is the ultimate morality of mind.
—ALFRED NORTH WHITEHEAD

BEYOND POLISH

It is easy to think that style is just the polish that makes a sentence more appealing, but more than appeal is at stake in choosing subjects and verbs in these two sentences:

1a. **Serbs and Albanians** DISTRUST each other because **they** HAVE ENGAGED in generations of cultural conflict.

1b. **Generations of cultural conflict** HAVE CREATED distrust between Serbs and Albanians.

Which sentence better reflects what really causes Serbs and Albanians to distrust each other—their deliberate actions, as in (1a), or, as in (1b), their history? Such a choice of subjects and verbs even implies a philosophy of human action: do we freely choose to act, or do circumstances cause us to? It is not a stretch to see in our choice of a subject and its verb a reflection of that age-old debate about free will and determinism.

So our choices of what character to tell a story about—people or their circumstances—involve more than ease of reading, even more than a philosophy of action, because such choices also have an ethical dimension.

The Ethical Responsibilities of Writers and Readers

In the last nine lessons, I have relentlessly emphasized the responsibility we owe our readers to be clear. But if we are responsible readers, we also have a responsibility toward writers to read hard enough to understand the genuine complexity of ideas that can't be expressed in Dick-and-Jane sentences. It would be impossible, for example, for an engineer to revise this into language clear to everyone:

> The drag force on a particle of diameter d moving with speed u relative to a fluid of density p and viscosity μ is usually modeled by $F = 0.5C_Du^2A$, where A is the cross-sectional area of the particle at right angles to the motion.

Most of us do work hard to understand—at least until we decide that a writer failed to work equally hard to help us reach that understanding, or, worse, has deliberately made our reading more difficult than it has to be. Once we decide that a writer was careless or thoughtless or lazy—well, our days are too few to spend them on those indifferent to our needs.

But that response to gratuitous complexity only reemphasizes our responsibility for our own writing, for it seems axiomatic that if we don't want others to impose carelessly complex writing on us, then we ought not impose it on others. If we are socially responsible writers, we should make our ideas no simpler than they deserve, but no more difficult than they have to be.

Responsible writers follow a rule whose more general theme you probably recognize:

> Write to others as you would have others write to you.

Few of us violate that principle deliberately. It's just that we are all so inclined to think that our own writing is clear that if our readers struggle to understand it, then the problem must be not our deep writing but their lazy reading.

But that's a mistake, because if you underestimate your readers' real needs, you risk losing more than their attention. You risk losing what writers since Aristotle have called a reliable *ethos*—the character that readers infer from your writing: does your writing make them think you are difficult or accessible? amiably candid or impersonally aloof? trustworthy or deceitful?

Over time, the ethos you project in individual pieces of writing settles into your reputation. So it's not just altruistically generous to go an extra step to help readers understand. It's pragmatically smart, because we tend to trust most a writer with a reputation for being thoughtful, reliable, and aware of her readers' needs.

But there is more at stake here than even reputation. What is at stake is the ethical foundations of a literate society.

An Ethic of Style

We write ethically when as a matter of principle, we would trade places with our intended readers and experience what they do as they read our writing. None of us wants to hack through gratuitously unclear writing, so it seems self-evidently unethical to impose that kind of writing on others. Unfortunately, it's not quite that simple. How, for example, do we think about those who write opaquely without knowing they do; or those who knowingly write that way but defend it?

Unintended Obscurity   Those who write in ways that seem dense and convoluted rarely think they do, much less intend to. For example, I do not believe that the writers of this next passage *intended* to write it as unclearly as they did:

> A major condition affecting adult reliance on early communicative patterns is the extent to which the communication has been

> planned prior to its delivery. Adult speech behaviour takes on
> many of the characteristics of child language, where the commu-
> nication is spontaneous and relatively unpredictable.

> —E. Ochs and B. Schieffelin, *Planned and Unplanned Discourse*

That means (I think),

> When adults speak spontaneously, they rely on patterns of child
> language.

The authors might object that I have oversimplified their meaning, but those eleven words express what I remember from their
forty-four, and what really counts, after all, is not what we understand *as* we read, but how well we remember it the next day.

The ethical issue here is not those writers' willful indiffer-
ence, but their innocent ignorance. In that case, when writers
don't know better, readers who do (as you now do, I hope) have
the duty to meet another term of the reader-writer contract: we
must not just read carefully, but when given the opportunity, respond candidly and helpfully. I know many of you think that
right now you do not have the standing to do that. But one day,
you will.

Intended Misdirection

The ethics of writing are clearer when a writer knowingly uses
language in self-interested ways.

Example #1: Who Made the Mistake?   For example, a few
years ago, the Sears Company was accused of overcharging for
automobile repairs. It responded with an ad saying:

> With over two million automotive customers serviced last year in
> California alone, mistakes may have occurred. However, Sears
> wants you to know that we would never intentionally violate the
> trust customers have shown in our company for 105 years.

In the first sentence, the writer avoided mentioning Sears as the
party responsible for mistakes. He could have used a PASSIVE
verb:

> . . . mistakes **may have been made.**

But that would have encouraged us to wonder "By whom?" Instead, the writer found a verb that moved Sears off stage by saying mistakes just "occurred," seemingly on their own.

In the second sentence of that ad, though, the writer focused on *Sears,* the specific responsible agent, because he wanted to emphasize its good intentions.

> **Sears** . . . would never intentionally violate . . .

If we revise the first sentence to focus on Sears and the second to hide it, we get a very different effect:

> When we serviced over two million automotive customers last year in California, we made mistakes. However, you should know that no intentional violation of 105 years of trust occurred.

That's a small point of stylistic manipulation, innocent of any malign motives. This next one is more significant.

Example #2: Who Pays the Bill?   Consider this letter from a natural gas utility telling me and hundreds of thousands of other customers that it was raising our rates. (The topic/subject in every clause, main or subordinate, is boldfaced.)

> **The Illinois Commerce Commission** has authorized a restructuring of our rates together with an increase in Service Charge revenues effective with service rendered on and after November 12, 1990. **This** is the first increase in rates for Peoples Gas in over six years. **The restructuring of rates** is consistent with the policy of the Public Utilities Act that **rates for service to various classes of utility customers** be based upon the cost of providing that service. **The new rates** move revenues from every class of customer closer to the cost actually incurred to provide gas service.

That notice is a model of misdirection: after the first sentence, the writer never begins a sentence with a human character, least of all the character whose interests are most at stake—me, the reader. He (or perhaps she) mentions me only twice, in the third person, never as a topic/agent/subject:

> . . . for service to various classes of utility **customers**

> . . . move revenues from every class of **customer**

The writer mentions the company only once, in the third person, and not as a responsible topic/agent/subject:

> . . . increase in rates for **Peoples Gas**

Had the company wanted to make clear who the real "doer" was and who was being done to, the notice would have read more like this:

> According to the Illinois Commerce Commission, **we** can now make you pay more for your gas service after November 12, 1990. **We** have not made you pay more in over six years, but under the Public Utilities Act, now **we** can.

If the writer *intended* to deflect responsibility, then we can reasonably charge him with breaching the First Rule of Ethical Writing, for surely, he would not want that same kind of writing directed to him, systematically hiding who is doing what in a matter close to his interests.

Example #3: Who Crashes?   Finally, here is a passage that raises an even greater ethical issue, one involving life and death. Some time ago, the Government Accounting Office investigated why more than half the car owners who got recall letters did not comply with them. The GAO found that car owners could not understand the letters or were not sufficiently alarmed by them.

I received the following. It shows how writers can meet a legal obligation while evading an ethical one (I number the sentences):

> [1]A defect which involves the possible failure of a frame support plate may exist on your vehicle. [2]This plate (front suspension pivot bar support plate) connects a portion of the front suspension to the vehicle frame, and [3]its failure could affect vehicle directional control, particularly during heavy brake application. [4]In addition, your vehicle may require adjustment service to the hood secondary catch system. [5]The secondary catch may be misaligned so that the hood may not be adequately restrained to prevent hood fly-up in the event the primary latch is inadvertently left unengaged. [6]Sudden hood fly-up beyond the secondary catch while driving could impair driver visibility. [7]In certain circumstances, occur-

rence of either of the above conditions could result in vehicle crash without prior warning.

(When asked what make of car the letter refers to, I dodge the question.)

First, look at the subject/topics of the sentences.

¹a defect	²this plate	³its failure
⁴your vehicle	⁵the secondary catch	
⁶sudden hood fly-up	⁷occurrence of either condition	

The main character/topic of that story is not me, the driver, but my car and its parts. In fact, the writers ignored me almost entirely (I am in *your vehicle* twice and *driver* once) and omitted all references to themselves. In sum, it says,

There is a car that might have defective parts. Its plate could fail and its hood fly up. If they do, it could crash without warning.

The writers—probably a committee of lawyers—also nominalized verbs and made others passive when they referred to actions that might alarm me:

failure	vehicle directional control	heavy brake application
be misaligned	not restrained	hood fly-up
left unengaged	driver visibility	warning

If the writers intended to deflect my fear and maybe my anger, then they violated their ethical duty to write to me as they would have me write to them, for surely they would not swap places with a reader deliberately lulled into ignoring a condition that threatened his life.

Of course, being candid has its costs. I would be naive to claim that we are all free to write as we please, especially when a writer's job depends on protecting an employer's self-interest. Maybe the writers of that letter felt coerced into writing it as they did. But that doesn't mitigate the consequences. When we knowingly write in ways that we would not want others to write to us, we abrade the trust that sustains a civil society.

We should not, of course, confuse unethical indirectness with the human impulse to soften bad news. When a supervisor says "I'm afraid our new funding didn't come through" we know it means "You have no job." But that indirectness is motivated not by dishonesty, but by kindness.

It is important to note where these writers focused their attention. They chose the subject/topics of their sentences carefully to deflect attention from themselves and from their reader (me). Our choice of subjects is crucial not only when we want to be clear, but also when we want to be misleading.

Rationalizing Opacity

A more complicated ethical issue is how we should respond to those who know they write in a complex style, but claim they must, because they are breaking new intellectual ground. Are they right, or is that just self-serving rationalization? This is a vexing question, not just because we can settle it only case-by-case, but because we may not be able to settle it at all, at least not to everyone's satisfaction.

Here, for example, is a sentence from a leading figure in contemporary literary theory:

> If, for a while, the ruse of desire is calculable for the uses of discipline soon the repetition of guilt, justification, pseudo-scientific theories, superstition, spurious authorities and classifications can be seen as the desperate effort to "normalize" *formally* the disturbance of a discourse of splitting that violates the rational, enlightened claims of its enunciatory modality.

—Homi K. Bhabha

Is that the expression of a thought so complex, so nuanced that what it says can be expressed only as written? Or is it babble? How do we decide whether in fact his nuances are, at least for ordinarily competent readers, just not accessible, given the time most of us have for finding them?

We owe readers an ethical duty to write precise and nuanced prose, but we ought not assume that they owe us an indefinite amount of their time to unpack it. If we choose to write in ways that we know will make readers struggle—well, it's a free country. In the marketplace of ideas, truth is the prime value, but not the only one. Another is the time it takes to extract it.

At the end of the day, I can suggest only that when writers claim their prose style must be difficult because their ideas are new, they are, as a matter of simple fact, more often wrong than right. The philosopher of language Ludwig Wittgenstein said,

> Whatever can be thought can be thought clearly; whatever can be written can be written clearly.

I'd add a nuance:

> Whatever can be written can usually be written *more* clearly, with just a bit more effort.

Salutary Complexity/Subversive Clarity

There are two more defenses of complexity: one claims that complexity is good for us, the other that clarity is actually bad.

As to the first claim, some argue that the harder we must work to understand what we read, the more deeply we must think and the better we will understand. Everyone should be happy to know that no evidence supports such a claim, and substantial evidence contradicts it.

As to the second claim, some argue that "clarity" is a device wielded by those in power to mislead us about who really controls our lives. By making things deceptively simple, they say, those who feed us information oversimplify it, rendering us unable to understand the full complexity of our political and social circumstances. Here is an example:

> The call to write curriculum in a language that is touted as clear and accessible is evidence of a moral and political vision that increasingly collapses under the weight of its own anti-intellectualism. . . . [T]hose who make a call for clear writing synonymous with an attack on critical educators have missed the role that the "language of clarity" plays in a dominant culture that cleverly and powerfully uses "clear" and "simplistic" language to systematically

undermine and prevent the conditions from arising for a public culture to engage in rudimentary forms of complex and critical thinking.

—Stanley Aronowitz, *Postmodern Education*

He makes one good point: language is deeply implicated in politics, ideology, and control. In our earliest history, the educated elite used writing itself to exclude the illiterate, then Latin and French to exclude those who knew only English. More recently, those in authority have relied on a vocabulary thick with Latinate nominalizations and on a Standard English that requires those Outs aspiring to join the Ins to submit to a decade-long education, during which time they are expected to acquire not only the language of the Ins, but their values, as well.

Moreover, clarity is not a natural virtue, corrupted by fallen academics, bureaucrats, and others jealous to preserve their authority. Clarity is a value that is created by society and that society must work hard to maintain, for it is not just hard to write clearly. It is almost an unnatural act. It has to be learned, sometimes painfully (as this book demonstrates).

So is "clarity" an ideological value? Of course it is. How could it be otherwise? But those who attack clarity as part of an ideological conspiracy to oversimplify complicated social issues are as wrong as those who attack science because some use it for malign ends: neither science nor clarity is a threat; we are threatened by those who use clarity (or science) to deceive us. It is not clarity that subverts, but the unethical use of it. We must simply insist that, in principle, those who manage our affairs have a duty to tell us the truth as clearly as they can. They probably won't, but that just shifts the burden to us to call them on it.

With every sentence we write we have to choose, and the ethical quality of those choices depends on the motives behind them. Only by knowing motives can we know whether a writer of clear prose would willingly be the object of such writing, to be influenced (or manipulated) in the same way, with the same result.

That seems simple enough. But it's not.

AN EXTENDED ANALYSIS

It's easy to abuse writers who manipulate us. It's more difficult to think about these matters when we are manipulated by those whom we would never charge with deceit. But it is just such cases that force us to think hard about matters of style and ethics.

The most celebrated texts in our history are the Declaration of Independence, the Constitution, and Abraham Lincoln's Gettysburg Address and Second Inaugural Address. In previous editions of this book, I discussed how Thomas Jefferson artfully manipulated the language of the Declaration and how Lincoln did the same in the Gettysburg Address. Here I examine his Second Inaugural Address.

Lincoln delivered it in March 1865, just before the end of the Civil War. He knew the North would win, but feared that it would punish the South for both slavery and the carnage of the war. As we have seen, he was right to worry. Anticipating that outcome, Lincoln tried to reconcile North and South in words engraved in our national memory:

> With malice toward none; with charity for all; with firmness in the right, as God gives us to see the right, let us strive on to finish the work we are in; to bind up the nation's wounds; to care for him who shall have borne the battle, and for his widow, and his orphan—to do all which may achieve and cherish a just, and a lasting peace, among ourselves, and with all nations.

We have, however, not committed to memory his opening sentences, because we are stirred by neither the elegance of their language nor the loftiness of their thought:

> Fellow-countrymen: At this second appearing to take the oath of the presidential office, there is less occasion for an extended address than there was at the first. Then a statement, somewhat in detail, of a course to be pursued, seemed fitting and proper. Now, at the expiration of four years, during which public declarations have been constantly called forth on every point and phase of the great contest which still absorbs the attention and engrosses the energies of the nation, little that is new could be presented.

> The progress of our arms, upon which all else chiefly depends, is as well known to the public as to myself; and it is, I trust, reasonably satisfactory and encouraging to all. With high hope for the future, no prediction in regard to it is ventured.

In fact, were that paragraph anonymous, we might judge it pedestrian, because it is as abstract and impersonal as the worst institutional prose. Lincoln could have written this:

> Fellow-countrymen: As **I appear** here for the second time to take the oath of the presidential office, **I** have less occasion to **address** you at length than **I** did at the first. Then **I** thought it fitting and proper that **I state** in detail the course to be pursued . . .

In fact, that is close to the style of his First Inaugural Address:

> Fellow-citizens of the United States: In compliance with a custom as old as the government itself, **I appear** before you to address you briefly, and to take before you the oath prescribed by the Constitution . . . **I** do not **consider** it necessary at present for me to discuss . . .

Or he could have written this:

> Fellow-countrymen: As **we** meet for this second taking of the oath of the presidential office, **we** have less need for an extended address than **we** had at the first. Then **we** felt a statement, describing in detail, the course **we** would pursue, would be fitting and proper . . .

And that is close to the style of the Gettysburg Address:

> Now **we** are engaged in a great Civil War, testing whether that nation, or any nation so conceived and so dedicated, can long endure. **We** are met on a great battlefield of that war. **We** have come to dedicate a portion of that field . . .

In fact, Lincoln seems so intent on impersonality that in his last sentence he dangled a modifier:

> **With high hope for the future,** no prediction in regard to it is ventured. [With high hope for the future, I do not venture to predict it.]

Either Lincoln dozed, or he had something else in mind.

In that first paragraph, the topics of his sentences deflect our attention from the participants and focus it on the event and his message (they are boldfaced):

> **this second appearing to take the oath of the presidential office,** there is . . .
>
> **a statement** . . . seemed fitting
>
> **public declarations** have been constantly called forth
>
> **little that is new** could be presented
>
> **The progress of our arms** . . . is . . . well known
>
> **it [progress of arms]** . . . is . . . encouraging to all.
>
> **no prediction** . . . is ventured.

Why did he choose such an impersonal style (assuming he actually made a choice)? We might understand better if we looked at the rest of the speech. As you read, notice his subjects/topic (boldfaced):

> On the occasion corresponding to this four years ago, **all thoughts** were anxiously directed to an impending civil war. **All** dreaded it— **all** sought to avert it. While **the inaugural address** was being delivered from this place, devoted altogether to saving the Union without war, **insurgent agents** were in the city seeking to destroy it without war—seeking to dissolve the Union, and divide effects, by negotiation. **Both parties** deprecated war, but **one of them** would make war rather than let **the nation** survive; and **the other** would accept war rather than let **it** perish. And **the war** came.
>
> **One eighth of the whole population** were colored slaves, not distributed generally over the Union, but localized in the southern part of it. **These slaves** constituted a peculiar and powerful interest. **All** knew that **this interest** was, somehow, the cause of the war. **To strengthen, perpetuate, and extend this interest** was the object for which **the insurgents** would rend the Union, even by war; while **the government** claimed no right to do more than to restrict the territorial enlargement of it. **Neither party** expected for the war the magnitude or the duration which **it** has already attained. **Neither** anticipated that **the cause of the conflict** might cease with, or even before, **the conflict** itself should cease. **Each** looked for an easier triumph and a result less fundamental and astounding. **Both** read the same Bible, and pray to the same

God; and **each** invokes His aid against the other. It may seem strange that **any men** should dare to ask a just God's assistance in wringing their bread from the sweat of other men's faces; but let **us** judge not, that **we** be not judged. **The prayers of both** could not be answered; **that of neither** has been answered fully. **The Almighty** has His own purposes. "Woe unto the world because of offences! for it must needs be that offences come; but woe to that man by whom the offence cometh." If we shall suppose that **American slavery** is one of **those offences which** in the providence of God, must needs come, but which, having continued through His appointed time, **He** now wills to remove, and that **He** gives to both North and South, this terrible war as the woe due to those by whom **the offence** came, shall **we** discern therein any departure from those divine attributes which **the believers in a Living God** always ascribe to Him? Fondly do **we** hope—fervently do **we** pray—that **this mighty scourge of war** may speedily pass away. Yet, if **God** wills that **it** continue until **all the wealth piled by the bondman's two hundred and fifty years of unrequited toil** shall be sunk, and until **every drop of blood drawn with the lash** shall be paid by another drawn with the sword, as was said three thousand years ago, so still **it** must be said, "**the judgments of the Lord**, are true and righteous altogether."

With malice toward none; with charity for all; with firmness in the right, as **God** gives us to see the right, let **us** strive on to finish the work **we** are in; to bind up the nation's wounds; to care for **him who** shall have borne the battle, and for his widow, and his orphan—to do all which may achieve and cherish a just, and a lasting peace, among ourselves, and with all nations.

In the first sentence of the second paragraph, Lincoln continues the impersonal style of his introduction, both nominalized and passive:

On the occasion corresponding to this four years ago, **all thoughts** were . . . directed to an impending civil war.

He could have written *everyone was thinking of an impending civil war.*

Then for two short clauses, he switches to the simplicity we expect:

All dreaded it—**all** sought to avert it.

But in the next sentence, he adopts the impersonal passive again:

> While **the inaugural address** was being delivered . . .

But then he returns to the direct, subject/agent–verb/action style for several sentences (note, however, that the subjects are general, not specific):

> **insurgent agents** were in the city seeking to destroy it
>
> **Both parties** deprecated war
>
> **one of them** would make war
>
> **the other** would accept war
>
> And **the war** came.

(How can war just "come"? How else could he have expressed that idea?)

He then writes an oddly awkward passive sentence about slavery:

> **One eighth of the whole population** were colored slaves, not distributed generally over the Union, but localized in the southern part of it.

This would have been more direct:

> **Slaves** were one eighth of the population, most of them in the South.

In the indirectness of his sentence, Lincoln seems to hold slavery at a distance. He does the same in the next two sentences. They begin clearly, but toward their ends, they slip into impersonality:

> **These slaves** constituted a peculiar and powerful interest.
>
> **All** knew that **this interest** was, somehow, the cause of the war.

(Why didn't he write, *All knew that slavery caused the war,* or even, *The South caused the war?*)

Most of the subjects and verbs in the rest of the sentences reflect the direct style that we associate with Lincoln, but note how indirectly he keeps referring to slavery (I italicize references to it and boldface subject/topics):

> **To strengthen, perpetuate, and extend** *this interest* was the object . . .
>
> **the insurgents** would rend the Union
>
> **the government** claimed no right to do more than to restrict *the territorial enlargement of it*
>
> **Neither party** expected for the war the magnitude or the duration
>
> **it** has already attained.
>
> **Neither** anticipated
>
> *the cause* **of the conflict** might cease
>
> **the conflict** itself should cease

(How can slavery and war just "cease"? How else could he have written that?)

At this point, Lincoln's style quickens through a series of short clauses that introduce God as a character, not yet as an active agent, but as a passive object of prayers and requests (references to God are italicized):

> **Each** looked for an easier triumph
>
> **Both** read the same Bible, and pray to the same *God*
>
> **each** invokes *His* aid against the other.
>
> **any men** should dare to ask a *just God's assistance* in wringing their bread from the sweat of other men's faces
>
> let **us** judge not

Then in three short passive clauses, Lincoln implies that God can act, but has not yet acted as either side has prayed:

> that **we** be not judged [by God?]
>
> **The prayers of both** could not be answered [by God];
>
> **that of neither** has been answered fully.

Lincoln then returns to his direct active style, naming God in the subject of four of the next eleven clauses as an acting, purposeful agent:

The Almighty has His own purposes.

If **we** shall suppose that

American slavery . . . must needs come

He now wills to remove

He gives to both North and South this terrible war

shall **we** discern therein any departure from those divine attributes

the believers in *a living God* always ascribe to *Him?*

Fondly do **we** hope—fervently do **we** pray

this mighty scourge of war may speedily pass away.

Yet, if *God* wills that

it continue until

all the wealth piled . . . toil shall be sunk,

every drop of blood . . . shall be paid by another

the judgments of *the Lord*, are true

Then the majestic climax we all remember:

> With malice toward none . . . let **us** strive on to finish the work we are in . . .

In other words, once Lincoln gets past that first abstract and in-direct paragraph and a half, he demonstrates what we take to be his classic American prose style: clear, candid, simple, and direct.

With one striking and powerful exception.

Of all the sentences crafted by American writers, none, I think, is craftier than this one, the longest in the speech, by far the most complex, and certainly the most important:

> If we shall suppose that American slavery is one of those offences which in the providence of God, must needs come, but which, hav-ing continued through His appointed time, He now wills to re-move, and that He gives to both North and South this terrible war as the woe due to those by whom the offence came, shall we dis-cern therein any departure from those divine attributes which the believers in a living God always ascribe to Him?

In that seventy-eight-word sentence Lincoln implies that the North has no right to punish the South for the war, because the war was given by God:

> **He** gives to both North and South this terrible war . . .

Nor can the North take credit for ending slavery. God did that, too:

> **He** now wills to remove [this offence of American slavery]

And (as Lincoln implies a few sentences later) it will not be a triumphant North that ends the war, but God, at a time of His own choosing:

> If **God** wills [to] continue [the war]

In other words, the North has no right to punish the South for the war or to take credit for ending it or slavery: it's all God's doing. That's the whole point of the speech. It justifies its great last sentence.

But before he made God responsible for the war and for ending both it and slavery, he wrote this oddly indirect passage about slavery's origin:

> **American slavery** is one of those **offences which** in the providence of God, must needs come

It echoes other phrases: *the war came, cause of the conflict might cease,* and, *the conflict itself should cease.* It all seems to happen on its own.

That clause about slavery is ambiguous in two ways. First, how are we to parse the phrase *American slavery?* Is *American* the agent of slavery as in *Americans enslave Africans,* or its victim, as in *Americans are enslaved?* Or is it both?

Second, how should we parse the verb *continued?*

> . . . one of those offences . . . which, having continued through His appointed time, He now wills to remove

It could mean *the offence of slavery continued through His appointed time,* or it could mean *God continued the offense of slavery through His appointed time.* Which is it? Or is it both?

But what really distinguishes this passage is its nominalizations. There are only five in these seventy-eight words, a strikingly low proportion for a dramatic speech. But three of them occur in just the first sixteen words: *slavery offence,* and *providence*. We could revise them into verbs and assign them subject/agents:

American **slavery**	→ Americans ENSLAVE Africans
is one of those **offences**	→ Americans OFFENDED God
which in the **providence** of God	→ God PROVIDES [something]

If we reassemble those clauses into a sentence, we get a startling claim:

> God provided that Americans enslave Africans, and that offended God.

Might we reasonably suppose that Lincoln thought a statement so direct would raise a theological issue so thorny that, at least on this occasion, he would just as soon avoid it?

To be sure, Lincoln believed that God had ordained every terrible thing that happened to both North and South. And he had no problem saying clearly that God *gave* the war to both sides, that God *willed* the end of slavery (as opposed to its just "ceasing," as he had written earlier), and though he prays the war will "pass away," he also knows that God might *will* it to continue.

But Lincoln seems unwilling to assign the origin of slavery to God. He uses direct verbs to express God's agency in bringing the war and ending both it and slavery, but he nominalizes verbs that would make God responsible for slavery, then buries that agency and action in the middle of the sentence (*in the providence of God*). Lincoln seems to want it both ways: God is responsible for everything, including slavery, but he doesn't want to say so.

That seventy-eight-word sentence is, I think, the stylistic *tour de force* of American literature.

But what does that have to do with his impersonal opening paragraph? Perhaps this: Lincoln believed that the enormity of the war was God's doing and that both North and South had earned God's punishment. In fact, the only time he refers to North or South by name, he makes them the object of God's wrath:

> He gives to both North and South this terrible war . . .

He made all the other subject/topic/agents nonspecific, even vague: *agents, parties, one, the other, both, all, each, neither, any man.* In fact, Lincoln seems deliberately to avoid assigning any action to any specific agent, until he introduces God as the Ultimate Agent.

And perhaps that explains the impersonality of that opening paragraph. Knowing he would later focus on God as the only specific agent in the story of the Civil War, Lincoln wanted to create an indefinite, impersonal blue/gray–gray/blue background of minor players to subordinate their—and his—role in American history to God's direct agency.

It is a great speech, especially that last sentence whose words are part of our national conscience. Even the parts that feel uninspired now seem at least explicable.

But now recall the question that motivated this discussion. What are we to make of these stylistic sleights-of-hand, of the hypercomplexity of that key sentence? How do we judge the way Lincoln (what word do we use here—manipulates? handles? manages?) shapes the responses of his audience? In so doing, was he unethical? The easy answer is no, and I think that's right, at least if we judge by his intentions. But the question forces us to think hard about the ethic of clarity as an unqualified, foundational value. At the crucial moment in his speech, Lincoln was not clear, and, I think, deliberately and rightly so.

SUMMING UP

How, finally, do we decide what counts as "good" writing? Is it clear, graceful, and candid, even if it fails to achieve its end? Or is it writing that does a job, regardless of its integrity and means? We have a problem so long as *good* can mean either ethically sound or pragmatically successful. We resolve that dilemma by our First Principle of Ethical Writing: we write well when we would willingly experience what our readers do when they read what we've written. That puts the burden on us to imagine our readers and their feelings.

If you are even moderately advanced in your academic or professional career, you've experienced the consequences of unclear writing, especially when it is your own. If you are in your early years of college, though, you may wonder whether all this talk about clarity, ethics, and ethos is just so much finger wagging. At the moment, you may be happy to find enough words to fill three pages, much less worry how clear they are. And you may be reading textbooks that have been heavily edited to make them clear to first-year students. So you may not yet have experienced much carelessly dense writing. But it's only a matter of time before you will.

Some wonder why they should struggle to learn to write clearly when bad writing seems so common and has no cost. What experienced readers know, and you eventually will, is that clear and graceful writers are so few that when we find them, we are desperately grateful for them. They do not go unrewarded.

I also know that for many writers the pleasure of crafting a good sentence or paragraph is often just in the achievement of it, for its own sake. It is an ethical satisfaction some of us find not just in writing, but in everything we do: we take pleasure in doing good work, no matter the job. It is a view expressed by the philosopher Alfred North Whitehead, with both clarity and grace:

> Finally, there should grow the most austere of all mental qualities; I mean the sense for style. It is an aesthetic sense, based on admiration for the direct attainment of a foreseen end, simply and without waste. Style in art, style in literature, style in science, style in logic, style in practical execution have fundamentally the same aesthetic qualities, namely, attainment and restraint. The love of a subject in itself and for itself, where it is not the sleepy pleasure of pacing a mental quarter-deck, is the love of style as manifested in that study. Here we are brought back to the position from which

we started, the utility of education. Style, in its finest sense, is the last acquirement of the educated mind; it is also the most useful. It pervades the whole being. The administrator with a sense for style hates waste; the engineer with a sense for style economizes his material; the artisan with a sense for style prefers good work. Style is the ultimate morality of mind.

—Alfred North Whitehead, *The Aims of Education and Other Essays*

Index